THE DEVELOPMENT OF A RATIONALE AND MODEL PROGRAM TO PREPARE TEACHERS FOR THE BILINGUAL-BICULTURAL SECONDARY SCHOOL PROGRAMS

FREDERICO M. CARRILLO

San Francisco, California
1977

Published by

R AND E RESEARCH ASSOCIATES
4843 Mission Street, San Francisco   94112

Publishers
Adam S. Eterovich
Robert D. Reed

Library of Congress Card Catalog Number
77-081 021

81- 5006
ISBN
0-88247-473-1

ACKNOWLEDGEMENTS

Mil gracias al "Institute for Cultural Pluralism" y a su fundador, Dr. Manuel Reyes Mazón, cuya ayuda, dirección y estímulo ha hecho este estudio posible.

Deseo expresar mi agradecimiento a mi colega de trabajo y amiga, Joyce Laeser por sus sugerencias, redacción y estímulo. Muy agradecido también de las muchas horas de trabajo de la mecanógrafa Mary Ann O'Meara.

Muchísimas gracias a los miembros de mi comité--Dr. Robert H. White, Dr. Leopoldo Macías y el Dr. Rupert Trujillo. Estoy especialmente agradecido del Dr. Robert H. White por su persistente ánimo y fé en mí.

Agradezco mucho la paciencia y entendimiento que han demonstrado mi esposa e hijas durante la preparación de este estudio.

Por fin, mil gracias a mi madrina, Dora S. Medina, por la redacción final.

CONTENTS

TABLES

FIGURES

CHAPTER I

INTRODUCTION

Traditionally, cultural, ethnic and linguistic differences have been equated with inferiority and second class citizenship in the United States. The results promulgated by this attitude have been that minority group children have had to assimilate into the Anglo culture at the expense of learning how to be ashamed of their parents and of their cultural and historical heritage. America has equated the speaking of English and Anglo-American values with patriotism and good citizenship and has regarded bilingualism as an enormous liability.

In comparison, citizens of other nations value multilingualism and multiculturalism for its significant political, social, economic and educational consequences. In the developing nations of the world, the demand for language pluralism has been caused by the rise in the status of one or more of the vernacular languages combined with the need to maintain an international language for the purposes of education and commerce. In other nations where the official language has already attained international status, a changing climate of tolerance toward minorities has often made it possible for ethnic groups speaking a language other than that of the national majority to organize with official approval their own schools in their own language.

There are few countries where one cannot find instances of bilingualism. In the past decade the demand for bilingualism has been increasing in most parts of the world. Fishman (1968) stated that about 50 percent of the world population is bilingual in varying degrees but that here in the United States only certain types of bilingualism have been considered "good" in the past. Many Americans have long been of the opinion that bilingualism is "a good thing" if acquired via travel, but that it is "a bad thing" if acquired from one's parents or grandparents. Spanish in the United States, for example, is a prestige idiom only where there are small numbers of Spanish-speakers. In areas where Spanish-speakers comprise a relatively large group, it is a language held in considerable contempt. Fishman (1966) noted this attitude in the United States with respect to most diverse ethnic languages. He concluded that as long as these languages and cultures are truly "foreign" our schools will accept them. However, when they are found in their own backyards, the schools deny them.

Fishman (1966), in documenting the efforts of various ethnic and religious groups to maintain their mother tongue and culture, provided for the first time a full picture of the extent and complexity of American multilingualism. An earlier study by Fishman (1965) provided specific information concerning the effect of bilingualism in the United States. Some 19 million Americans do not speak English as their mother tongue. There are 500 non-English publications in the United States with a circulation of five and a half million. About 1,600 radio stations broadcast non-English programs 6,000 hours weekly. Two-thirds of the total hours are devoted to Spanish language broadcasts. There are 1,800 ethnic cultural organizations in the United States, and approximately 3,000 ethnic group schools, more than half of which offer instruction in the ethnic language.

Countless children fall into the group whose language is different from the majority. If we take the world as a whole, then we are indeed dealing with a general problem. Fishman and Luder (1973) have pointed out the consequences of this situation:

> Given a moment's thought it is quite apparent that most of the world's school children . . are not taught to read and write the same language or variety that they bring with them to school from their homes and neighborhoods. Indeed if this phenomenon if viewed historically, the the

1

discrepancy between home language and school language increases dramatically the further we go back in time into periods that predate the vernacularization of education and mass education itself.

Within the United States the problem seems considerably smaller than when viewed from an international perspective. However, it has been greatly complicated by the fact that it has been ignored for so long. Only since the advent of the Bilingual Education Act of 1967 has much attention been focused on the problem that there are languages other than English spoken in the United States, and that many children come to school speaking a language other than English.

Background of the Problem

The result of the Bilingual Education Act and the consequent recognition and attention given to cultural and linguistic diversity in the United States has been the implementation of a large number of bilingual and bilingual-bicultural education programs in public schools with bilingual student populations. In New Mexico, for example, the total number of such programs has now reached 100.

The implementation of these programs, however, brought into focus yet another educational problem. It became apparent quite rapidly that, in order to teach in, develop curriculum and plan strategies for bilingual-bicultural education programs, very specialized skills were necessary--skills which were not provided in the regular teacher preparation programs offered at universities and colleges. In the early stages of bilingual-bicultural education, many teachers and administrators were highly frustrated by the lack of trained personnel to carry out the objectives set forth for their programs. Because of the lack of adequate preparation programs, there was a crucial shortage of teachers trained specifically for bilingual-bicultural education. As a result, administrators were forced to resort to shifting bilingual teachers, that is, speakers of English and Spanish, from their regular assignments to bilingual programs. In most cases these teachers were undereducated in linguistic and cultural skills and almost entirely unprepared for the highly specialized task of teaching in a bilingual-bicultural program. It is no wonder that many teachers often felt unequal to the task and that many of the programs were somewhat less than successful.

In a report prepared for the National Conference on Educational Opportunities for Mexican Americans, Angel (1968) discussed the inappropriateness of selecting teachers for bilingual-bicultural programs solely on the basis of a familiarity with the Spanish and English languages. He also pointed out the need for specialized language skills in the following statement:

A rather interesting point of view exists regarding teachers for the elementary schools' programs, namely, that there are plenty of Spanish-speaking teachers in all states of the Southwest who can be the teachers of Spanish, regardless of whether they have special training or not. Such an idea is an error that can smash the teaching-of-Spanish programs on the rocks of faddism and ineptness.

In the first place, it is questionable that all elementary teachers of Mexican-American descent can and do speak Spanish fluently enough. The tremendous emphasis on the learning of English and the lack of interaction with Mexico and other Latin American countries, has gradually caused many Mexican-American teachers to forget the Spanish they once knew. In the second place, many teachers who will still speak Spanish fluently simply have no notion of the linguistic composition of their own language. Thirdly, especially for those programs in which Spanish is to be the language of instruction, the lack of knowledge (combined with the lack of material) of Spanish language arts on the part of the teacher, will lead to chaos, or more disastrously, to poor education for the pupils. Fourthly, modern linguistic approaches require special training in theory and practice.

It has become increasingly apparent that the teacher who speaks two languages is not necessarily an effective bilingual-bicultural teacher. According to Valencia (1972), even specialized preservice training is not enough to provide all the necessary skills. He advocated inservice training as well for continued expansion of skills:

> Merely being bilingual does not necessarily mean that a teacher has knowledge or can exhibit teaching skill in a bilingual instructional program, and therefore inservice programs are needed in schools targeted for bilingual instruction. Providing prospective teachers with the opportunity to develop bilingual instructional skills in a preservice training program will facilitate placement in a bilingual instructional program. However, it should not be assumed that any teacher has reached ultimate growth in teaching performance. School systems must consider the notion of providing inservice activities to faculties in terms of individual needs.

Another factor which influenced the ineffectiveness of bilingual-bicultural programs in the past was that some of the teachers, although representatives of the same language and culture group, had reached a degree of assimilation in the mainstream culture which made them insensitive to the problems of their Spanish-speaking students. This situation jeopardized the objectives of the bilingual-bicultural programs.

The fifth report of the U.S. Commission on Civil Rights (1973), which focused on the differences in teacher interaction with Mexican American and Anglo students, found that Mexican American teachers tended to use the relatively few Anglos in their classrooms to emphasize the middle-class Anglo culture and values to the Mexican American students. It was concluded that, to a large extent, many Mexican American teachers operated under the philosophy that success for Mexican American students lay in acquiring Anglo traits. This phenomenon was relfected in statistics which showed the relative amounts of praise and encouragement given to Anglo and Mexican American students by their teachers. Although the statistics revealed that both Anglo and Mexican American teachers gave more approval to Anglo students than to Mexican American students, the discrepancy was most marked when it was measured for Mexican American teachers.

Carrillo (1973), on the basis of observations made of teachers who were actually working in bilingual-bicultural programs and attending special summer institutes to improve their skills, found that these teachers were unskilled in techniques to incorporate appropriate referents in the teaching of history and culture of the Southwest. Furthermore, he found that in addition to a lack of basic language skills and vocabulary, they were lacking in basic knowledge of southwest history and cultures.

Angel (1968), Aragon (1971), Carter (1970), and Ulibarri (1971) have all concluded in their studies that training in cross-cultural understanding, the relationship between culture and behavior, and the ability to communicate on many different levels are all essential for bilingual-bicultural teachers. These skills are considered essential in addition to a general understanding of the specific cultural and historical background of the students being taught.

In essence, the experience of the first decade of bilingual-bicultural education has taught that very specialized and comprehensive teacher preparation must be an integral part of the implementation of successful bilingual-bicultural programs in the public schools. In order to cope with the many problems that were encountered in the early stages of these programs, special training programs were initiated.

In April of 1970 the Educational Professional Development Act (EPDA) allocated funds to the New Mexico State Department of Education for the purpose of providing training for bilingual-bicultural elementary teachers. Under the direction of Henry W. Pascual, Director of Communicative Arts in the State Department of Education,

3

Bilingual-Bicultural Teacher Training Institutes were conducted during the summers of 1970, 1971 and 1972. Pascual (1969) established the following priorities regarding teachers' needs for the instructional phase of the Institutes:

1. Complete Spanish language immersion.
2. Instruction in the writing system of the Spanish language.
3. Structured oral language development.
4. Practice in oral and silent reading in Spanish.
5. Instruction in History of the Southwest in Spanish.
6. Instruction in Spanish language grammar suitable for elementary school teaching.
7. Learning in the area of teaching Spanish language arts, mathematics, science, social studies in Spanish for the third grade level.
8. Instruction in teaching English as a second language.
9. Total cultural immersion.

The EPDA Institutes provided one of the first steps in eradicating many of the problems which bilingual-bicultural education programs had encountered. Of the more than 100 elementary teachers and administrators who received training in the Institutes, many are presently engaged in teaching bilingual-bicultural programs and are sharing their training with other teachers. Others are serving as directors, coordinators and teacher trainers in bilingual programs and are providing preservice and inservice training to classroom teachers in these programs.

Need for the Study

Much positive change has occurred in the preparation of teachers for bilingual-bicultural education programs. Several universities and colleges in New Mexico and throughout the nation have taken the initiative to implement some phases of teacher training in bilingual-bicultural education. The present philosophy in our institutions of higher education is, however, to initiate, develop and promote teacher training programs for bilingual-bicultural education only for the elementary level of schooling. Little consideration or long-range planning to articulate bilingual-bicultural educational needs throughout the entire educational process has been effected.

Perhaps this implies that bilingual-bicultural education should be forgotton altogether on the secondary level, thus eliminating Spanish as a language of instruction in the classroom and maintaining its foreign language status for all, disregarding the students' level of familiarity and/or proficiency in the language. Possibly this further implies that educators feel that the interest in and study of other cultures and languages is detrimental to the students' ability to function effectively in an "American society" and should cease with the elementary level. More likely, however, is the theory that the failure of bilingual-bicultural education to permeate all phases of education is the result of a lack of understanding of the total concept of bilingual-bicultural education and the positive effects the implementation of such a concept can have on all the children of the United States.

In essence, a bilingual-bicultural education program should not be viewed as a compensatory program solely for the benefit of minority group students. Furthermore, it should not be considered as a transitory vehicle to facilitate assimilation into the mainstream culture. A sound program should work to preserve the rich cultural heritage of the linguistically and culturally different and simultaneously provide children from the mainstream culture with a second language and culture. Effective bilingual-bicultural programs should provide the opportunity for all children in the schools to become bilingual-bicultural. A bilingual-bicultural

4

program should include long-range plans established on a practical basis as well as on measurable objectives. The ultimate goal should be to institutionalize this philosophy of education throughout the entire educational program. Jaramillo (1972), an advocate of this philosophy, has stated:

> Bicultural education, although old in the world at large, is a new concept in this country. Its history is yet to be written. Its future can be bright. Bicultural education is a legitimate educational program for everyone, and it should not be viewed as a remedial, compensatory, or special education program. When viewed from this negative perspective, it is doomed toward failure. We also need constant reminders that although many children enrolled in bicultural programs are poor, it is not an anti-poverty program. All children enrolled in bicultural programs will benefit. But there must be a genuine commitment toward cultural pluralism in the schools where these programs are started; they cannot be commenced solely because there are federal monies available. The concept must be a part of the American system and continue forward as an integral part. Only with this philosophy does bicultural education have a bright future. Otherwise, it continues the parche mal pegado syndrome. ("Patch work" responses to the needs of the Mexican American student.)

Fortunately, as bilingual-bicultural education on the primary level of schooling matures, it is gradually beginning to reach into the intermediate and secondary level. In New Mexico, for example, a great number of schools now have bilingual-bicultural programs which have reached the intermediate grades. A 1972-1973 survey of the existing and proposed bilingual-bicultural programs in New Mexico, conducted by the Bilingual-Bicultural Communicative Arts Unit, revealed that approximately 46 schools would offer bilingual-bicultural education on the intermediate level during the 1973 academic year. Table 1 provides a list of these schools and the grade levels in which they provide instruction. As the table indicates, most of these programs are in the lower elementary levels, especially fourth, fifth and sixth grades. Most of these programs, however, have plans to expand as the students in them advance to the junior and senior high grades. Two junior high schools (Gadsden and East Las Vegas) and two senior high schools (Belen and East Las Vegas) have already implemented some components of bilingual-bicultural education in their curricula.

In view of the fact that bilingual-bicultural education seems inevitable on the secondary level in New Mexico, it is imperative to begin now to prepare for it. It should be apparent that the needs of primary and elementary students differ from those of junior and senior high school students. Therefore, the preparation programs, curriculum development, and teaching strategies which have evolved over the years for the lower grades will not be adequate for the implementation of successful secondary programs. If the problems which were encountered in the early stages of bilingual-bicultural education on the primary and elementary level are to be avoided, a comprehensive and effective program needs to be developed now to prepare teachers for the forthcoming bilingual-bicultural secondary school programs.

Nature of the Study

The purpose of this study will be to develop a bilingual-bicultural teacher preparation program for the secondary level. The designation bilingual-bicultural, rather than multilingual-multicultural, conveys the particular focus of this program on the two major cultural groups of the Southwest, Mexican Americans and Anglos. The design of the program will be based primarily on an assessment of the teacher skills considered essential for working with Mexican American students since their special needs have been neglected for so long by traditional teacher preparation programs.

Table 1

SURVEY OF INTERMEDIATE AND SECONDARY BILINGUAL-BICULTURAL PROGRAMS IN NEW MEXICO 1972-1973

School District	Schools	Grade Level
Albuquerque	Coronado	6
	Riverview	5
	Griegos, San Felipe, San José	4
Artesia	Rose Lawn, Yucca	5
Belen	Belén Senior High	11, 12
Bernalillo	Roosevelt, Cochiti	5
Chama	Chama Elementary, Tierra Amarilla	4
Espanola	Española Elementary	4
Gadsden	Gasden Junior High	8
Grants	San Rafael	6
	Cubero, San Mateo, Seboyeta, Sierra Vista	5
Hagerman	Hagerman Elementary	4
Hobbs	Edison	6
Las Cruces	Mesilla, Lucero	6
	Zía Junior High, Alameda Junior High	7
East Las Vegas	Las Vegas City Schools	1-12
West Las Vegas	Armijo, North Public, South Public Union, Valley, Villanueva	4
Lovington	Llano, Jefferson	4
Pecos	Pecos Elementary	4
Penasco	Peñasco Elementary	4
Portales	Linsey	6
Questa	Questa Elementary, Costilla	6
Santa Fe	Agua Fría, Alvord, Larragoite	4
Santa Rosa	Antón Chico	6
	Santa Rosa Elementary	4
Silver City	Sixth Street	4
Tucumcari	Zía	4

Source: New Mexico State Department of Education, 1972-1973.

It will also consider, however, those skills necessary for working with all kinds of children in any bicultural or multicultural setting. It is important to remember when developing any bilingual-bicultural program either for teacher preparation or for public school students that no one cultural group lives in a vacuum. In the long run, the success of bilingual-bicultural education will be determined by its ability to contribute to a society where tolerance and harmony prevail and where all diverse groups regard each other with respect.

The first phase of the study examines the special educational needs of the Mexican American student. In order to assess the needs of the Mexican American from the perspective of his current achievement and status both in and out of school, an extensive profile of the Mexican American in the Southwest is outlined. An examination of the demographic features of the Mexican American population, based on the 1970 Census of Population, establishes its concentration in the Southwest of the United States in numbers great enough to merit special attention from educational institutions. A careful review of statistics provided by the U.S. Commission on Civil Rights, Report 11, (1971) relative to the educational achievement of Mexican American students in the Southwest and other related literature reveals significant information about the areas and levels of schooling in which Mexican Americans are experiencing insufficient rates of achievement and a lack of full participation. A description of the socio-economic profile of the Mexican American in the Southwest includes an examination of the external restraints such as discrimination, segregation, and lack of encouragement for motivating upward social mobility both in and out of school which have affected the lack of educational and consequent socio-economic schievement of this group.

The second step in assessing the special educational needs of the Mexican American examines those educational practices and attitudes which have been the apparent causes of his failure to achieve in the past, in an effort to discover where change needs to take place. A brief historical perspective of the educational attitudes toward the Mexican American traces how attitudes and emphases have changed throughout this century. An examination of how current attitudes toward diversity, Spanish language, and Mexican American culture have affected the Mexican American student provides specific information on the factors which have alienated Mexican Americans from the educational process. Information is also provided on those educational areas, such as teacher preparation, testing instruments, school facilities and community involvement, which have influenced the Mexican American student's involvement in a relation to the educational process.

The assessment of the needs of the Mexican American student from the point of view of his overall achievement in society and the factors which have obviously affected this underachievement through a process of alienation leads this study into its second phase--an examination of the bilingual-bicultural education program as a solution to the Mexican American student's problems. This phase of the study examines the rationale given for bilingual-bicultural education by a number of educators in order to determine its relativity to the special needs of the Mexican American population and its benefits to society as a whole. In addition, this examination provides a look at the general scope of the definition of bilingual-bicultural education.

Going beyond the theoretical stage of bilingual-bicultural education, an examination is made of actual practices in bilingual-bicultural education programs; the way these programs can be integrated into the regular curriculum on the secondary level; and a brief review of the kinds of preparation offered for bilingual-bicultural education teachers in institutions of higher learning. In order to ascertain the current offerings in bilingual-bicultural teacher education, an extensive survey was conducted. The first stage of this survey involved contacting chief state school officials and teacher certification officers of the 50 states to determine which states had a person designated as State Program Director for Bilingual Education and/or special certification requirements for bilingual-bicultural education teachers. Those states identified were then recontacted to determine the nature and extent of the teacher training offered in those states.

Having established some of the needs of the Mexican American student and having examined bilingual-bicultural education as a solution to many of these needs, phase three of the study analyzes the opinions of a wide range of persons on the skills and competencies needed by teachers to provide successful educational experiences for Mexican American and other students in bilingual-bicultural education programs. A number of studies were conducted simultaneously to collect a wide variety of opinions on priorities in teacher preparation for bilingual-bicultural education:

1. An extensive review of current literature on teacher preparation in bilingual-bicultural education was carried out.

2. The survey of current bilingual-bicultural teacher preparation programs carried out in phase three was carefully analyzed to determine its priorities in terms of numbers and types of courses offered in various subject areas.

3. A number of bilingual-bicultural education related conferences were attended by the author, and the consensus of conference participants were collected and analyzed to determine their priorities in bilingual-bicultural teacher education.

4. An extensively circulated questionnaire prepared by the Institute for Cultural Pluralism at San Diego State University to solicit specific competencies considered essential for bilingual-bicultural education teachers from a wide range of community and educational interests was collected and analyzed to determine the priorities in teacher education of its respondents.

The fourth phase of the study presents a model undergraduate teacher preparation program in bilingual-bicultural education for the secondary level, based on a composite of the information gained in the previous three phases. The description of the model program includes a rationale; the general objectives of the program; specific objectives and minimum criteria for students in the program; a general description of the program, suggested course work and course descriptions.

Organization of the Remainder of the Study

Chapter II presents a profile of the Mexican American in the Southwest. This profile includes a demographic picture of the Mexican American, a review of the educational achievement of the Mexican American student, and an examination of the socio-economic status of the Mexican American in the Southwest.

Chapter II presents the apparent causes for the lack of sufficient achievement by Mexican American students. It examines such factors as negative attitudes toward culture and language and diversity in general. It also documents a lack of awareness on the part of the educational system that the Mexican American student has specialized and particular needs as distinguished from the needs of students from the mainstream population.

Chapter IV explores a possible solution to the educational problems confronted by the Mexican American student. In so doing, it examines the rationale for bilingual education, describes the nature of the bilingual-bicultural education program; and presents the present status of programs to prepare teachers for bilingual-bicultural education programs.

Chapter V reviews the relevant literature regarding the competencies needed by teachers in bilingual-bicultural education programs, identifies teacher competencies which universities and colleges are focusing on, and more importantly identifies the specific competencies regarded as essential by educators throughout the Southwest.

Chapter VI deals with the development of an undergraduate program for teachers in the bilingual-bicultural secondary school program. It is specifically designed for the New Mexico area.

Chapter VII provides conclusions drawn as a result of the total study and presents the recommendations of the author.

Summary

As the number of bilingual-bicultural education programs in New Mexico grows and as established programs process their students through the elementary grades, plans are being formulated to expand the scope of these programs to the junior and senior high grade levels. Experience in the implementation of elementary bilingual-bicultural programs has pointed to the crucial need to provide carefully planned goals and adequately trained personnel to carry out these goals well in advance of actually implementing the programs. The need for teachers with very specialized and sophisticated skills to implement successful bilingual-bicultural programs has been well established.

This study is designed with the goal of developing a teacher training program for bilingual-bicultural education on the secondary school level. In this manner, when the forthcoming secondary bilingual-bicultural programs are ready to be implemented, there will be available professional personnel equipped to realize their goals.

The model program which is outlined in this study is based on a thorough investigation of the problems which Mexican American students have faced in the past and a careful analysis of a composite of information relating to the kind of competence which is needed by teachers to carry out an effective bilingual-bicultural education program. The overall goal of the model program is to incorporate a philosophy of cultural pluralism which affirms that bilingual-bicultural education should be an integral part of the total educational process and that it is beneficial to all students in the school system.

CHAPTER II

A PROFILE OF THE MEXICAN AMERICAN IN THE SOUTHWEST

In order to begin the development of a model for bilingual-bicultural teacher
education, it is first necessary to look at the population it will serve to determine
its characteristics and needs. This chapter presents information about the demographic characteristics of the Mexican American population in the United States in an
effort to show its importance in terms of size as well as where the population is
concentrated. An examination of the deficient educational achievement of the Mexican American in the Southwest gives clear evidence of the failure of the traditional
educational system to provide equal opportunity for this large group of Americans.
It is impossible to separate poor educational achievement from an inadequate rate of
social advancement and economic achievement. A look at the socio-economic profile of
the Mexican American in the Southwest, along with a discussion of the discrimination
and segregation practiced against this group, serves to bring out a cause-effect
relationship between deficient educational achievement and a low rate of socio-
economic advancement. The evidence presented in this chapter emphasizes the crucial
need to provide innovative programs which will break this cycle and make equal opportunity for Mexican Americans a reality.

Demographic Characteristics of the Mexican American Population

Data Collection Techniques

Julian Samora (1966) reported that, in the past, it has not been possible to get
an accurate picture of the size and composition of the Spanish-speaking population in
the United States. In 1930, the Bureau of Census attempted to enumerate the Spanish-
speaking population under a "Mexican" heading: "All persons born in Mexico or having
parents born in Mexico who are definitely not White, Negro, Indian, Chinese, or
Japanese." Unfortunately, this definition excluded those whose grandparents, or even
more remote ancestors had come to the United States by way of Mexico. This report
accounted for 61,916 "Mexicans" in New Mexico, when as a matter of fact, according to
Samora (1966), the Spanish-speaking population numbered 200,000 or what was then half
the population of the state. The 1940 Bureau of Census substituted "Spanish-speaking"
for "Mexican" and asked, "What was the principal language other than English spoken in
your home during childhood?" This excluded many persons who identified themselves with
the Spanish-speaking group, but whose principal home language was English. The 1950
and 1960 censuses attempted enumeration by Spanish surname. This term has recently been
used to refer to the Mexican American population in the Southwest, although Samora
(1966) concluded that it was still an inadequate classification tool.
The 1970 census used four different identifiers of the population of Spanish
ancestry living in the United States. Each of these identifiers provided useful information about the people frequently referred to as "Spanish-speaking."
The first identifier was one which asked for the birthplace of the individual and
his parents. From these questions information was made available concerning the number of first and second generation immigrants from such countries as Mexico, Cuba and
Puerto Rico. About 5.2 million persons in the United States were reported to be of
Apanish birth or parentage using this identifier.
The second identifier classified persons of Spanish surname. In the five south-
western states, Arizona, California, Colorado, New Mexico and Texas, about 4.7 million

persons were identified as having a Spanish surname.

The third measure asked persons whether they considered themselves to be of Mexican, Puerto Rican, Cuban, Central or South American, or other Spanish origin. More than nine million persons answered that they belonged to one of these groups.

The fourth identifier asked for the language (mother tongue) spoken in the person's home in early childhood. Nearly eight million persons reported Spanish as that language. For purposes of the census report, all persons living in families in which the head of the family or wife reported Spanish as the mother tongue were included in this category, designated "persons of Spanish language." The total number listed in this category was about 9.6 million.

There has been much dissatisfaction from several sources as to the reliability of the 1970 census in regards to the Mexican American population in the United States. In April 1971 the Mexican American Population Commission of California pointed out the inaccuracy of the 1970 census statistics in its first official biannual report on the Spanish-Mexican American population in California. Eight months later, the United States Census Bureau accepted the findings of the Commission's report as a result of a federal district court charging the Census Bureau with haphazard methodology and indifference to Mexican Americans.

Due to the lack of Mexican American Population Commissions in other states, however, this writer has had to resort to using the information provided in the 1970 Census of Population. Although the figures may not be completely without error, they do present a general picture of the size, distribution and source of the current Mexican American population suitable for this study. It is worthy of note that in the 1970 census Spanish-language forms were used for the first time for purposes of data collection. This new element along with the diversification of classification instruments ensures more accuracy in the 1970 findings than in years past.

Results of the 1970 Census

Mexican Americans constitute the second largest minority group in the United States. Of the nine million Spanish surnamed residents counted in the 1970 census, 4,532,435 were categorized as Mexican American, although Nava (1971) has stated that there are probably more than five million Mexican Americans in the United States This ethnic group is concentrated largely in the American Southwest: Arizona, California, Colorado, New Mexico and Texas, with smaller enclaves in Nevada and Utah. There are also significant numbers of Mexican Americans in Michigan, Illinois, Indiana and Ohio. The 1970 census indicated that the Mexican American population in these states amounted to 282,555 persons.

Of the total Mexican American population, 87 percent inhabited the southwestern states. According to the census, this ethnic group constituted 11 percent of the total population of these states. California and Texas, each having 3.4 million Mexican American residents each, together held 77 percent of the entire Mexican American population in the Southwest.

In 1970, 82 percent of the Mexican Americans were American born. Their median age, 19.3 years, was ten years younger than the median age of the total population and 4.1 years younger than the median age of all non-whites. One out of every five children in the Southwest was a Mexican American. Mexican Americans were reported to be the fastest growing minority group in the United States. This is attributed in part to a natural increase in births and also to continuing immigration from Mexico. Table 2 provides figures for the pattern of immigration to certain key states from Mexico to the United States during the period 1968-1972. The influx of migrants into the United States is really a separate factor in these statistics since it is seasonal in nature; however, many of these migrants are reamining as permanent residents of the United States.

One important characteristic of the Mexican American population revealed in the 1970 census was its concentration in major urban centers. Figures indicated that about

11

80 percent of the Mexican American persons listed resided in urban areas. According to Andersson and Boyer (1970) this is a relatively new phenomenon. They cited as an example a school in Chicago where the Spanish-speaking enrollment rose from 300 to 3,000 in just two years. One probably conclusion to be drawn is that, although the major portion of the Mexican American population has moved into urban areas, they may still retain many characteristics of rural populations.

The demographic information presented here indicates that we are concerned with a sizable group of Americans. Our system of education has been a key element in the past in enabling children of various ethnic backgrounds to grow and develop into full parti- cipation in American life. During the great waves of immigration to the United States in the late 19th and early 20th centuries, society turned to the schools as the princi- pal instrument for assimilating these groups into the American mainstream. By and large, the schools succeeded in accomplishing this enormous task.

In the Southwest, however, where the Mexican American has been a resident since the 16th century, the schools have failed to fulfill their traditional role of assimi- lation into the American economic mainstream. The fact that one out of every five children in the Southwest recorded in the 1970 census was a Mexican American is reason enough for institutions of higher learning and public schools to provide programs and personnel to serve the needs of this area's largest culturally distinct group. An examination of the educational profile and the socio-economic profile of the Mexican American proves that, in the past, this has not been the case.

Deficient Educational Achievement of the Mexican American

Only 75 percent of the Mexican American children of school age are in school according to Andersson and Boyer (1970). Only one-third of the students of high school age are actually attending high school. One-half of the Mexican American school popu- lation is concentrated in the first three grade levels. Fifty-five percent of the pupils beyond the first grade are two years behind their grade level. Spolsky (1972) has reported that the dropout rate among Mexican Americans is one of the highest in the United States. Strom (1965) has concluded that the schools in their insistence on programs and standards that the Mexican American considers unrelated to his life or that doom him to unending successions of failure precipitate his desire to aban- don his educational endeavors at the first opportunity. He further stated:

> Every year a significant number of basically sound young Americans
> discover that they are not really wanted and that neither their teachers
> nor their curricula experiences seem to pay any attention to who they
> are, what they have and what they have not and what they can do and what
> they cannot. Instead, imposed upon them is a nonsensical experience which
> goes under the name of education.

Without exception, minority students achieve at a lower rate than Anglos. Their academic success is poorer, their repetition of grade is more frequent, and they parti- cipate in extra-curricular activities to a lesser extent than do their Anglo peers.

In presenting a comprehensive profile of the deficient educational achievement of the Mexican American student, this study will examine the Mexican American student with regard to five standard measures devised by the U.S. Civil Rights Commission (1971): School Holding Power, Reading Achievement, Grade Repetition. Overageness, and Parti- cipation in Extracurricular Activities. In addition, a sixth factor, the median years of schooling completed by Mexican Americans, will also be examined.

Table 2

NUMBER AND PERCENTAGE OF IMMIGRANTS FROM MEXICO TO UNITED STATES
IN KEY STATES FOR PERIOD 1968-1972[1]

State	Number of Immigrants	Percentage of Total
California	79,335	45.4
Texas	50,363	28.8
Arizona	23,822	13.6
New Mexico	1,469	0.8
Colorado	988	0.5
Illinois	16,370	9.3
Michigan	1,294	0.7
Indiana	749	0.4
TOTAL	174,390	100

Source: Annual Reports of Immigration and Naturalization Service 1968-72.

[1] These figures do not include all the states which experienced immigrants from Mexico during this period; however, the states listed do account for the major portion of immigrants.

School Holding Power

Among three major ethnic groups of the Southwest, Anglo, Mexican American and Black, Mexican Americans have the highest rate of attrition before high school graduation. As Table 3 indicates, the loss begins earlier among Mexican Americans than other groups. By the eighth grade, nine percent of Mexican Americans have already left school. At the time of high school graduation, only 60.3 percent of those who started first grade are still in school. Among Blacks, of every 100 youngsters entering first grade, 98.6 percent attend the eighth grade, but only 66.8 percent receive high school diplomas. In contrast, of every 100 Anglos who enter the first grade, nearly all attend the eighth grade, and 87 percent finish high school.

The gap in the holding power between Anglo pupils and members of the two minority groups widens in the college years. While nearly one out of every two Anglo students who begins school can expect to enter college, only about one in every four Mexican Americans and Blacks can expect to do so. If the public schools of the Southwest maintain their present low rates of holding power with minority students, large numbers will not receive even the minimum high school education and only a handful will receive a college diploma.

Table 3

SCHOOL HOLDING POWER FOR ANGLOS, MEXICAN AMERICANS, AND
BLACKS IN FIVE SOUTHWESTERN STATES

State	Percentage in Grade 1 All Groups	Percentage in Grade 8			Percentage in Grade 12			Percentage to Enter College			Percentage to Finish College		
		Anglo	M.A.	Black	Anglo	M.A.	Black	Anglo	M.A.	Black	Anglo	M.A.	Black
Arizona	100	99.2	96.5	94.6	88.9	81.3	71.6	53.5	33.0	29.3			
California	100	100.0	93.8	97.3	85.7	63.8	67.3	46.9	29.2	24.0			
Colorado	100	100.0	99.0	100.0	94.8	67.4	70.9	50.6	14.6	*			
New Mexico	100	96.9	93.4	92.7	79.4	71.1	67.6	52.9	22.2	24.8			
Texas	100	100.0	91.1	98.8	85.1	52.7	64.4	53.0	16.2	26.7			
TOTAL SOUTHWEST	100	100.0[1]	91.1	98.6	86.0	60.3	66.8	49.3	22.5	28.8	23.8	5.4	8.3

* Number too small for analysis

Source: U.S. Commission on Civil Rights, The Unfinished Education, Report II (October, 1971).

[1] This is the figure which appears in the report; however, according to this writer's calculations, a more accurate figure is 99.2.

14

Reading Achievement

The imporatnce of reading is widely acknowledged by educators as a means of determining academic achievement. Reading ability is crucial and indispensible for success and progress in other academic subjects. Marland (1970) emphasized the importance of reading when he stated:

> . . .we must as a nation, discover ways to teach all mentally adequate citizens to read. Even at the expense of the (other) programs this essential function of civilized man must have preeminence in our priorities. Otherwise, our best intentions in other social interventions, such as job development, equal opportunities, housing, welfare and health will have only passing and peripheral effect.

As the figures in Table 4 reveal, in the southwestern states 50 to 70 percent of Mexican American and Black students in fourth, eighth and twelfth grades are reading below the level expected for these grades. In comparison, only 25 to 34 percent of all Anglo youngsters in these grades are reading below grade level. This means that twice as many students of minority groups as Anglos are below average in reading performance.

In two states, New Mexico and Texas, the situation for the Mexican American student does not seem to deteriorate as badly by grade twelve. It must be remembered, however, that the schools have failed to hold many of those students whose reading performance was the poorest in the lower grades. Thus, the improvement in reading achievement from grade eight to grade twelve in these states is merely an illusion.

Grade Repetition

Most grade repetition occurs in the first grade for the Mexican American, as Table 5 indicates. Some 16 percent of these students repeat the first grade as compared to six percent of the Anglo students. Although the disparity between Mexican American students and Anglo students is not as wide in the fourth grade, Mexican American students are still twice as likely to repeat this grade as their Anglo peers.

It is interesting to note that the two states with the largest Mexican American student populations, Texas and California, reveal significant differences in repetition rates for first grade. The figures for Texas represent the highest repetition rate recorded at 22.3 percent, while the figures for California are among the lowest at less than 10 percent.

Overageness

Another measurement directly linked to grade repetition is the overageness of pupils in relation to assigned grade level. Mexican Americans in the Southwest are as much as seven times as likely to be overaged as their Anglo classmates as the figures in Table 6 illustrate. The most significant difference appears in the eighth grade where more than nine percent of the Mexican American pupils are overaged as compared to little more than one percent of the Anglo students. In the Southwest the degree of overageness increases for Anglos and Blacks throughout the schooling process, but actually decreases for Mexican Americans between eighth and twelfth grades. The reason for this phenomenon is that a large percentage of overaged Mexican Americans leave school before graduation. It is estimated that at least 42 percent of overaged Mexican Americans do no continue in school through the twelfth grade.

Table 4

PERCENTAGE OF ANGLO, MEXICAN AMERICAN AND BLACK STUDENTS
READING BELOW GRADE LEVEL IN FIVE SOUTHWESTERN STATES

	Grade 4			Grade 8			Grade 12		
State	Anglo	M.A.	Black	Anglo	M.A.	Black	Anglo	M.A.	Black
Arizona	25.0	43.6	55.4	32.8	65.5	64.7	49.1	74.6	76.9
California	27.0	52.1	55.0	27.1	57.2	55.0	34.1	62.8	58.7
Colorado	25.5	56.7	61.9	33.0	55.1	64.8	23.1	59.1	64.8
New Mexico	24.9	48.1	51.6	35.1	58.4	56.7	33.9	53.7	74.3
Texas	21.0	51.8	59.0	27.5	73.5	63.9	30.9	64.7	71.7
TOTAL SOUTHWEST	25.3	51.3	55.9	28.2	64.2	58.3	33.7	62.6	69.7

Source: U.S. Commission on Civil Rights, The Unfinished Education, Report II (October, 1971).

16

Table 5

PERCENTAGE OF ANGLO, MEXICAN AMERICAN AND BLACK STUDENTS
REPEATING FIRST AND FOURTH GRADES IN FIVE
SOUTHWESTERN STATES

State	Grade 1			Grade 4		
	Anglo	M.A.	Black	Anglo	M.A.	Black
Arizona	5.7	14.4	9.1	0.8	2.7	0.7
California	5.6	9.8	2.2	1.6	2.2	1.0
Colorado	3.9	9.7	7.7	0.7	1.7	1.3
New Mexico	8.5	14.9	19.0	0.9	4.2	1.0
Texas	7.3	22.3	20.9	2.1	4.5	5.1
TOTAL SOUTHWEST	6.0	15.9	8.9	1.6	3.4	1.8

Source: U.S. Commission on Civil Rights, The Unfinished Education, Report II,
(October, 1971).

Table 6

PERCENTAGE OF ANGLO, MEXICAN AMERICAN AND BLACK STUDENTS TWO OR MORE
YEARS OVERAGE IN FIVE SOUTHWESTERN STATES

State	Percentage in Grade 1			Percentage in Grade 4			Percentage in Grade 8			Percentage in Grade 12		
	Anglo	M.A.	Black	Anglo	M.A.	Black	Anglo	M.A.	Black	Anglo	M.A.	Black
Arizona	0.7	2.5	1.5	1.2	5.6	1.3	1.1	11.8	3.0	1.4	10.9	5.5
California	0.9	1.7	0.7	0.7	2.1	0.7	0.8	2.3	0.3	0.1	2.3	1.9
Colorado	0.7	2.1	0.9	0.5	2.3	0.7	0.6	1.5		2.5	3.9	5.4
New Mexico	0.4	1.7		2.7	5.5	2.0	2.3	10.8	1.8	1.7	6.8	9.1
Texas	0.7	6.6	3.2	1.3	12.0	6.1	2.1	16.5	6.7	4.9	10.5	4.6
TOTAL SOUTHWEST	0.8	3.9	1.2	1.0	6.9	1.8	1.2	9.4	2.1	1.4	5.5	4.4

Source: U.S. Commission on Civil Rights, The Unfinished Education, Report II, (October, 1971).

18

Participation in Extracurricular Activities

Students often learn as much from contacts with their classmates as they do from their textbooks. Extracurricular activities provide students with special opportunities to expand their personal and intellectual horizons and such activities as student government will encourage students to develop qualities of leadership and respect for the democratic process. Involvement in extracurricular activities makes school more meaningful and enhances school holding power.

Table 7 presents a comparative view of the percentage of Anglo and Mexican American students who have held positions of leadership or social recognition in a number of extracurricular activities. Figures are shown for schools where Anglos constitute the majority of the student population and schools where Mexican American students constitute the majority. As Table 7 illustrates, Mexican American students are underrepresented in these positions even in schools where they constitute a majority of the student body.

Median Years of Schooling Completed

An examination of the median years of schooling of the Mexican American 25 years of age and over in comparison with the total population, as shown in Table 8, reveals a great disparity in the educational achievement of the Mexican American and the achievement of the population as a whole.

In every state of the Southwest the median years of schooling completed by the total population exceeds twelve years. The highest median years of schooling completed by Mexican Americans 25 years of age and older is achieved in California, where the median is 8.8 years or 28 percent below the median years completed by the total population of the state. The lowest median for Mexican Americans, 6.3 years, is found in Texas and is 47 percent lower than the median years of schooling completed by the total population in that state. In the Southwest as a whole, the median years of schooling for the Mexican American 25 years of age and over is four years below that of the total population or 34 percent below average.

A look at the median years of schooling completed by adult Mexican Americans, those 25 years of age and over, compared with Mexican Americans 14 years of age and over allows some room for optimism. The latter group has a median of 1.2 grade levels higher than the former group. This is indicative that the situation is slowly improving. However, the fact that 40 percent of Mexican American students have left school by grade twelve (see Table 3) means this is still a matter of concern.

Implications

Under all six measurements of school achievement examined, minority students are performing at significantly lower levels than Anglos. These wide disparities are matters of crucial concern to the nation and of special concern to this study. Testifying before the Senate Select Committee on Euqal Educational Opportunities, Obledo (1970) stated his views on the educational inequities experienced by Mexican Americans:

> The Mexican American has a lower educational level than either the Black or Anglo; the highest dropout rate; and the highest illiteracy rate. These truths stand as massive indictments of either negligent or intended homicide against a minority group. In essence, what this system has done is smother the soul and the spirit of an entire people.

19

Table 7

PERCENTAGE OF EXTRACURRICULAR ACTIVITY POSITIONS OF LEADERSHIP AND SOCIAL RECOGNITION HELD BY ANGLO AND MEXICAN AMERICAN STUDENTS IN SECONDARY SCHOOLS IN THE SOUTHWEST

Item	Schools Having Mexican American Enrollments			
	Less than 50%		Greater than 50%	
	Anglo	M.A.	Anglo	M.A.
Percentage of Total Student Enrollment	72.8	17.4	19.2	74.5
Percentage to Hold Position As:				
Student Body President	79.2	8.6	34.3	65.7
Student Body Vice-President	79.0	10.5	35.3	61.8
Class President	73.0	14.4	26.8	60.8
Newspaper Editor	76.3	15.2	35.5	60.0
Homecoming Queen	74.3	18.2	23.1	73.1
Homecoming Queen Court	75.9	14.2	29.1	68.0
Cheerleader	75.7	12.8	44.9	50.2
Average Percentage of Above	76.2	13.4	32.7	62.8

Source: U.S. Commission on Civil Rights, The Unfinished Education, Report II (October, 1971).

Table 8

MEDIAN YEARS OF SCHOOLING COMPLETED BY MEXICAN AMERICANS
14 YEARS OF AGE AND OVER, MEXICAN AMERICANS 25 YEARS
OF AGE AND OVER, AND BY TOTAL POPULATION IN FIVE
SOUTHWESTERN STATES

State	Median Years of Schooling Completed		
	Total Population	Mexican Americans 25 Years of Age and Over	Mexican Americans 14 Years of Age and Over
Arizona	12.5	8.3	9.6
California	12.3	8.8	9.4
Colorado	12.6	8.7	9.4
New Mexico	12.1	8.3	9.2
Texas	12.1	6.3	8.7
TOTAL SOUTHWEST	12.3	8.1	9.3

Source: 1970 Census of Population.

Statistics indicate that the school holding power begins to deteriorate drastically for Mexican Americans between the eighth and twelfth grades. These are the years when these students are most sensitive and most concerned with an awareness of themselves, their shortcomings and their achievements. These are crucial years in the education of the Mexican American; years when the traditional American educational system has failed and continues to fail to reach the students. The apparent conclusion is that what is needed is another teaching approach for the Mexican American on the secondary level. As rodriguez (1968) has stated, the time has come for the school to recognize that it must change its program to fit the needs of the student rather than trying to punish the student for failure to fit the school.

Effects of External Restraints on the
Socio-Economic Profile of the Mexican American

External restraints imposed upon Mexican Americans have helped to maintain for them a subordinate position in society. The external restraints which have resulted in the disproportionately low rate of advancement in the social and economic spheres described below can be seen in the form of the lack of motivation and adequate opportunity for upward mobility and a tradition of discrimination, stereotyping and segregation.

As indicated earlier, it is difficult to separate the factors which affect the socio-economic status of the Mexican American from those which affect his academic achievement. It is hoped, however, that an examination of how some of these restraints directly relate to the potential for social and economic upward mobility will make even clearer the role that effective programs on the secondary level can play in eradicating these restraints.

Socio-Economic Status of the Mexican American

The 1970 census revealed that Spanish surnamed people have consistently lower employment levels and that a greater percentage of this ethnic group live in poverty conditions then do Anglo Americans. For example, while only 12.6 percent of Anglos live in poverty conditions, 24.3 percent of Mexican Americans do. The Blacks have an even worse situation with 33.6 percent of them living in poverty conditions. In 1970 the median family income for the Spanish-speaking person was $7,334 as compared to $9,867 for Americans as a whole. Table 9 shows the percentage of all White, Mexican American and Black families in each income bracket from under $1,000 to over $50,000. The figures show that while only 56.6 percent of White families earn less than $12,000 annually, 72.1 percent of Mexican American families fall into this range. This results in only 27.9 percent of the families of Spanish-speaking persons earning over $12,000 a year in contrast to 43.4 percent of the White families in the United States.

The concentration of Mexican Americans in the low economic sector has prompted many Mexican Americans to drop out of school at an early age to help contribute to the support of their families. For youths from such families, a college education--indeed, a high school education--is a great luxury. Those who do graduate from high school often find themselves economically ineligible to go on to college.

The second report by the U.S. Civil Rights Commission (1971) revealed that, in the schools it surveyed, not only were minority students less likely than Anglos to finish high school, but also those who graduated were much less likely to go on to college. Principals in the schools surveyed estimated that in 1968, 37 percent of Mexican American graduates, 43 percent of Black graduates, and 57 percent of Anglo graduates went on to college. The obvious result of this is, of course, that Mexican Americans, unable to go on to college or even finish high school, are not in a good position to find prestigious and high paying jobs, thus perpetuating a cycle which could easily carry over to the next generation.

Table 9

INCOME DISTRIBUTION OF WHITE, SPANISH AMERICAN, AND BLACK FAMILIES IN THE UNITED STATES IN 1970

Annual Income Per Family	Percentage of White Families	Percentage of Span. Am. Families	Percentage of Black Families
Under $1,000	2.0	2.9	4.8
$1,000-$1,999	2.1	3.1	4.8
$2,000-$2,999	3.3	4.4	7.1
$3,000-$3,999	4.1	5.6	7.4
$4,000-$4,999	4.3	6.1	7.1
$5,000-$5,999	4.7	6.6	7.3
$6,000-$6,999	5.1	7.4	7.8
$7,000-$7,999	5.7	7.8	7.5
$8,000-$8,999	6.2	7.8	7.0
$9,000-$9,999	6.2	7.3	6.1
$10,000-$11,999	12.9	13.1	10.5
SUBTOTAL	56.6	72.1	77.4
$12,000-$14,999	15.6	13.0	10.9
$15,000-$24,999	21.3	12.6	10.2
$25,000-$49,999	5.5	2.0	1.3
$50,000 and Over	1.0	.3	.2
SUBTOTAL	43.4	27.9	22.6
TOTAL	100.0	100.0	100.0

Source: 1970 Census of Population.

Although no extensive study has been made of the Mexian American in relation to social class stratification, indications are that a small number of Mexican Americans can be truly called upper class. The vast majority of the Mexican Americans in the Southwest belong to the lower class. In studying the Mexican Americans, Ulibarri (1969) found them to be scattered over the occupational range. There were educated scholars and professionals as well as illiterate and unskilled laborers. Though this range is found in all other groups as well, Mexican Americans were particularly prone to be overrepresented in the lower occupational levels.

Ulibarri found further that another phenomenon differentiating Mexican Americans from Anglo Americans is the relative status and prestige accorded the Mexican American by the majority group. Invariably the majority group relegates lower status and prestige to the people in the minority group.

Potential for Upward Mobility

Concerning self-actualization among Mexican Americans, all of the variables regarding social class spelled out one important factor; namely, that there are definite limitations placed on minority members educationally, economically and socially. Even though the Anglo world provides unlimited opportunity for upward mobility, the Mexican American finds himself limited in his access to the statuses he can attain and the roles he can play in the Anglo world.

In school the student learns that through hard work, perserverance and luck he can achieve unlimited success. The adult reality of success, however, is an entirely different story. Status and role allocations are determined by the majority group and only a limited number of Mexican Americans are allowed upward mobility. This creates a low motivational level for the Mexican American desiring to work hard and reap the rewards later.

The carry over of this paradox into the school system is a disproportionate number of Mexican Americans placed in vocational education programs in high school. This phenomenon is evident even though, as Mayeske (1967) has pointed out, Mexican American students have high educational and occupational goals. Mayeske further stated that there is evidence to indicate that lower class youths in general tend to be channeled toward vocational education and are not encouraged to go to college. This channeling appears to hit Mexican Americans particularly hard.

In an earlier study, Heller (1965) observed that only 20 percent of Mexican American students were participating in high school college preparatory curricula in comparison with about 50 percent of the Anglo American students. The small number of Mexican Americans receiving college preparatory training may have a serious effect on the college holding power. The figures shown earlier in Table 3 reveal that while 22.5 percent of the Mexican Americans who begin first grade enter college, only 5.4 percent actually finish college. The tendency to push vocational education as a general palliative for minority groups, irrespective of individual differences in ability and motivation, has not served either individual or societal needs.

A factor which seriously influences the motivation of Mexican American youth is that the vast majority of their parents are employed in lower level occupations. Because of this, Mexican American youth have little opportunity to learn about the availability of alternative jobs or what is required to qualify for them in order to attain their individual goals. Anderson and Safar (1971) through extensive interviews with community members and school personnel in two multicultural southwestern communities found an almost unanimous feeling that Spanish American and Indian children are less capable of schieving desirable goals and ultimately becoming productive members of society than are their Anglo peers. Such a situation is scarcely conducive to facilitating upward mobility.

Blair (1972) has confirmed that Mexican Americans have been largely isolated by class, residence and language from the educational and occupational realms they wish to enter. In his opinion, this isolation has resulted because of a lack of information that would aid them in making plans to secure their goals. This problem has been complicated by the lack of understanding of the bureaucratic procedures involved in working within the system in order to obtain favors from it.

Discrimination and Segregation

In discussing the profile of the Mexican American population, one cannot discount the factors of discrimination and segregation. Discrimination and enforced segregation have taken place in each of the southwestern states and specifically in communities where the Anglo population constituted the majority. The Mexican American has been discriminated against not only because of his low economic status but also for his language, his culture and his Catholic religion.

The effect of discrimination on the psychological make-up of the Mexican American is immeasurable. The effects of discrimination against the language and culture of the Mexican American will be discussed in the next chapter as they relate to performance of the Mexican American child in school. What is of concern here is the effect of discrimination combined with segregation on the socio-economic status of the Mexican American.

The ethnically mixed population of the Southwest has traditionally consisted of a hierarchy with Anglos on the top and Mexican Americans on the bottom. Cooke (1948) stated that before World War II, Mexican Americans in Southern California were frequently refused housing in Anglo neighborhoods, excluded from certain public facilities, such as swimming pools and restaurants, and denied employment because of their ethnic background.

In Texas, Mexican Americans have been deliberately segregated more than elsewhere in the Southwest. Taylor (1934) stated that in the Corpus Christi area, he found that restrictive covenants in deeds frequently prohibited the sale of property to Mexican Americans in Anglo sections of town. According to Madsen (1964) as late as 1961 segregated patterns of living continued to exist in South Texas communities. Madsen described the area as:

> . . .populated by both Anglo and Mexican Americans who live in separate residential districts divided by a highway or railroad tracks. Anglo isolation from the Mexican American is not only spatial but social. Virtually the only relationship between the two groups is economics . . .The predominant relationship . . .is that of an employer to an unskilled employee.

Anglo communities in Arizona have also viewed themselves as racially and economically superior to the Mexican American. McWilliams (1948) quoted an Arizona newspaper in the 1930's which described the situation as follows:

> . . .the Arizona Mexicans have been segregated from the more fortunate Arizoans, both as strangers belonging to an alien race of conquered Indians and as a person whose enforced status in the lowest economic level makes them less admirable than other people.

Conclusions

An examination of the Mexican American in the Southwest makes it clear that the Mexican American is not achieving success in the educational, social or economic spheres at a rate comparable to that of the Anglo. Furthermore, a cycle can be seen in this pattern of underachievement. Poor educational achievement and a low rate of socio-economic advancement are inextricably interwoven.

Since educational success forms the basis for all other forms of success, then it is in the educational system that the solution for breaking this cycle must be found. The statistics on school holding power past the eighth grade and the median years of schooling completed by Mexican Americans and factors affecting motivation and potential for upward socio-economic mobility all point to the secondary level of schooling as the place where change is needed most. The schools must first of all find ways to keep Mexican Americans in school during high school and secondly develop programs and attitudes which will ensure that Mexican American high school students have their potential channeled in upward directions. Both of these goals are essential if the current profile of the Mexican American is to improve.

As a first step in establishing what can be done to achieve these goals, Chapter III examines the apparent causes of the failure of the traditional educational system to meet adequately the needs of the Mexican American student.

CHAPTER III

APPARENT CAUSES OF THE EDUCATIONAL PROBLEMS OF THE MEXICAN AMERICAN

In dealing with members of minority groups who have migrated to the United States throughout its history, the traditional method of the educational system has been to Americanize these groups in order to facilitate assimilation into the economic mainstream. The "cut all ties and anglicize" approach to education has not produced adequate results for the Mexican American. Reinforcing the evidence presented in Chapter II on the lack of educational success by Mexican Americans, Ulibarri (1969) has pointed out:

> About the only thing that can truly be said about the education of the Spanish Americans today is that more and more numbers are attending school today than did just a few years ago. Very little can be said, by the way of improvement of educational practices in the education of these people and very little can be said of the educational attainment of these people when compared with the educational attainment of the people throughout the United States.

This chapter will present information on the apparent causes of the failure of the educational system to meet the needs of the Mexican American as a first step in arriving at new strategies and attitudes which will provide successful educational experiences for this group. A brief overview of the history of the attitudes of the educational system toward the Mexican American reveals that, although beginning in apathy and indifference, it is becoming more responsive to the cultural and linguistic needs of the Mexican American.

Despite these new trends in education, however, certain attitudes and practices traditional in the system must still be analyzed for their effect on the Mexican American student. First of all, the "melting pot" theory of assimilation, though now being refuted, still exists. An explanation of the detrimental effects of this theory is essential if the new sensitivity toward language and culture of minority groups is not to be used merely as a tool for eventual, total Americanization. Second, although the need for cultural sensitivity is now recognized and valued by most educators, a pattern of negative cultural stereotyping is still evident in practice. The same can be said of language sensitivity. Although teachers and administrators now acknowledge language as a crucial factor in the education of the Mexican American, negative attitudes still exist toward that language and its use in the classroom.

These negative attitudes toward the difference in language and culture of the Mexican American form a background which has led traditionally to a lack of sensitivity to the special needs of the Mexican American. As a result of this lack of sensitivity, a number of specific policies can be seen which have contributed directly to the lack of educational achievement by Mexican American students. Among these factors are teachers who are not adequately prepared to deal with the specialized needs of Mexican American students; curricula and testing instruments designed without consideration for the particular skills of this group; poor physical facilities, especially in schools where Mexican American students form the dominant population; and a lack of sensitivity to and involvement with the Mexican American community from which the students come.

Historical Perspective of the Education of Mexican Americans

In a study of the educational neglect of the Mexican American, Carter (1970) traced the slowly changing attitudes of the dominant group toward the educational needs of the Mexican American. He characterized the first period from 1920 to 1930 as one of indifference. Mexican Americans were regarded as outsiders who would never be able to participate fully in society. They were looked upon as a "child" race. Educational literature of the period emphasized the inadequacy of the child citing I.Q. scores as evidence of inferiority. As Carter stated:

> Frequently, attitudes were tinged with racial prejudice; the literature emphasized the differences between the two cultures rather than their similarities. The typically low intelligence test scores were used as evidence of innate inferiority. This in turn was used to justify the common place segregation in schools. Although some concern was expressed for the state of the Mexican Americans' health, most of the literature reveals little interest in his economic and educational plight.

Beginning with the late 1920's, the works of Merian (1928) in California, Manuel (1930) in Texas, and Tireman (1941) in New Mexico on the education of Spanish-speaking and Indian children focused their attention on the teaching of English to non-English speaking children. These children were considered to have a "language problem" and needed to be Americanized before total instruction could take place. This approach implanted a philosophy which is still very apparent today throughout the schools in the Southwest. According to Angel (forthcoming):

> The almost exclusive attention to the teaching of English to bilingual children has had the effect of producing a type of intellectual "tunnel vision" which has precluded attention from being given to other aspects of learning, such as the implications of the effects of "culture" on affective development as well as on cognitive development. The experience of Tireman is typical of most of the thinking which has been done in the past and is still current today in the education of bilingual children.

During the Depression Years, many Mexican Americans left the rural areas and migrated to the cities in search of work. The cities became increasingly aware of the problems experienced by Mexican Americans in adjusting to the demands of urban existence. Gould (1932) reported:

> The W.P.A. ameliorated the situation somewhat by building schools and establishing a number of vocational schools and Americanization programs. More important, educators during the 1930's and through the mid-1940's began to consider the school as an agency for the acculturation of the Mexican American. "Appropriate methods" to accomplish Americanization were recommended in the hope that it would change . . . Mexican American children from half-hearted Americans into law abiding and useful citizens.

Carter (1970) noted that school programs during the 1930's and 1940's emphasized vocational and manual training, the learning of English, health and cleanliness, thrift and punctuality. Segregation was recommended and commonly established. Although segregation of the Mexican American was never required by statute in any of the five southwestern states, it had been practiced not only in the schools of the region, but in other aspects of life as well, as was discussed in the previous chapter. Cooke (1948) reported that in California, for example, under a law enacted in 1885 and amended in 1893, it was possible to segregate Indians and Mongolians in the public schools. To many Anglo administrators, this provided justification for segregating Mexican Americans as well.

During the 1940's New Mexico showed considerably more concern for the Mexican American student than the other southwestern states. Carter (1970) indicated that special programs were established in Taos (Taos County Project) and in Nambe (Nambe Program) for the Spanish-speaking student.

A shortage of labor during World War II and the immediate postwar boom period prompted the United States Government to contract with Mexico for agricultural labor. Because of the discrimination practiced in some areas of Texas, the Mexican Government refused to allow Mexican nationals to work in those areas. As a result of that decision, Carter (1970) stated that the Texas Good Neighbor Commission was established and state education authorities were prompted to give more consideration to the educational needs of the children of Mexican descent.

Carter further stated that while most of the public was still ignorant of, or indifferent to, the needs of the Mexican American, reports of teachers' conferences during the 1940's and 1950's revealed a growing concern for meeting the needs of the Mexican American in the schools. Teachers who were attempting to develop new methods for teaching these children were beginning to recognize the need for greater understanding of the socio-cultural background of the children.

Austin, Texas, in 1946 was the scene of the First Regional Conference of the Spanish Speaking People of the Southwest. According to Carter (1970) this conference centered its attention on the problems of school attendance and low academic achievement and the imperative need to improve the low socio-economic status of the Mexican American. Discussion at the conference resulted in recommendations to end segregation and improve school facilities. In regard to new programs for Mexican American students, the conference recommended the development of relevant curriculum built around the Mexican American community, improved teacher training to create positive attitudes toward the minority culture, and increased efficiency in the teaching of English.

During the 1950's and 1960's the civil rights movement and the growing emphasis on the socio-economic problems of minority groups contributed to a growing concern for the Mexican American. There was an increasing tendency to associate his educational problems with his low socio-economic status.

Carter (1970) stated that in 1964 at the Orange County Conference on the Education of Spanish Speaking Children and Youth held in Garden Grove, California, emphasis was placed on the need for special teacher preparation, the undemocratic nature of de facto segregation, and the need for improvement in the teaching of English. This conference laid less stress on radical change of the curriculum or intercultural education and more on the need for including content on the cultural heritage of the Mexican American.

Recent activities are indicative of a positive upward trend. Since the advent of the Elementary and Secondary Act of 1965, several innovative projects have been initiated. In Pecos, New Mexico, a three-year program (1965-1968) was established to incorporate the study of Spanish as an integral part of the daily classroom activities in the elementary school. The outcome of this project was a positive psychological impact on the children involved in it. These children developed positive attitudes toward the study of Spanish and also an awareness of the vastness and richness of the Hispanic cultural heritage through the study of geography, children's literature and Hispanic society. Fernandez (1968) emphasized the importance of these results by stating:

> Children in Pecos have the unique opportunity and special privilege to grow and to form not only as normal children, without the complex of being Spanish but also as extraordinary children--children that will gain the knowledge of speaking English and Spanish correctly.

The annual conferences of the Southwest Council of Teachers of Foreign Languages from 1966 on, revealed an exclusive interest in the improvement of the education of the Spanish-speaking child. These conferences concentrated on detailing facts about bilingual education, offering pertinent suggestions to interested participants, and presenting proposals relative to all levels of education of the Mexican American student. An abstract put out by the National Bilingual Institute (1973) stated that the ideas emerging consistently from the interaction among participants included the need for pre-school education, community participation in schools and the development of new and innovative classroom practices. Participants in these conferences also stressed the importance of university involvement, state legislation, and federal support for the implementation and maintenance of bilingual education programs.

The 1966-1967 summer NDEA Institutes for Advanced Studies for Teachers of Spanish to the Spanish speaking initiated the retraining of teachers of Mexican American students. These were later followed by the EPDA Bilingual-Bicultural Institutes of 1970 to 1972 described in Chapter I. These retraining programs have motivated colleges and universities in the United States to implement special programs for the improvement of education for Mexican Americans.

In April 1970 a small group of Mexican American students, community leaders and educators from throughout the United States organized the National Education Task Force de la Raza for the purpose of addressing particular problems related to the education of the Mexican American. The Task Force has since conducted a series of training institutes in Texas, Colorado, New Mexico and California to encourage and guide community leaders in obtaining quality education for Mexican American children. They have conferred with officials in the United States Office of Education on numerous occasions and obtained their support for their stated goals. They have identified and recruited Mexican Americans for leadership positions in the field of education. Consultants with expertise in bilingual-bicultural education, counseling and guidance, and school administration have helped Mexican Americans initiate needed innovations.

Negative Attitudes Towards Diversity

Clearly the attitude of educators toward the Mexican American is becoming more positive, and there is a growing awareness that the ability to work with Mexican American students requires specialized training and skills. Although there is still much to be done, the educational system is becoming increasingly more receptive to accepting new ideas and implementing new programs. It is within this context that an examination of certain attitudes which have had a pejorative effect on the Mexican American is carried out.

Although the "melting pot" theory of assimilation and negative attitudes toward Mexican American language and culture are rapidly becoming a thing of the past, these views are still held by many people as valid. Therefore, an explanation of the detrimental effect on the Mexican American child of such attitudes and their resultant practices seems essential if such attitudes are to be eliminated completely. Such an explanation is indeed a prerequisite for establishing positive attitudes toward all aspects of Mexican American life and the benefits of multi-cultural society, which is after all, or should be, the goal of any bilingual-bicultural education program.

The "Melting Pot" Theory

The "melting pot" theory has been the traditional accepted model of society. The pervading idea of this theory of assimilation is that all cultures in the United States should fuse to becoming one common culture. It cannot be denied that with many cultural groups this theory has been applicable and workable. However, in the case of the Mexican or Spanish American, who has been a resident of this area since the early 16th century, adherence to this ethnocentric model has been largely responsible for the failure of the traditional system and the dominant society to respect the cultural and linguistic distinctness of this group. The same can be said for Black and Native Americans, both of whom have been unable to assimilate into the American mainstream with this model.

John and Horner (1967) have stated that inherent in the "melting pot" theory is the assumption that any socialization acquired before school should be undone by the school so that the child can be turned out in the common mold. Part of the present day turmoil we have witnessed on college and high school campuses is directly attributable to the ethnocentric philosophy and curricula of schools that offer only the "assimilate or perish" alternative for minorities and then employ scapegoating rationalizations for the subsequent minority failure and dropouts. Extreme unhappiness, resentment and bitterness have been the result of this philosophy for many culturally different groups. This is emphatically illustrated in the words of Luis Valdez of El Teatro Campesino quoted from Steiner's (1970) study:

> They say this is the melting pot. I wonder who invented the melting pot. Horrible term! You melt people down, God! It shouldn't be that way. Our country should be a place where the individual is sacred. We have so many sorts of people. Every man has his own heart. Who gives you the right to cut a man's heart and put it in a melting pot? There are beautiful things in our lives. We have had them in our past and we will have them again. We will create our own flowers and songs.

Valdez's reactions are chiefly due to the fact that educational programs have been committed to making Mexican Americans into the image of the Anglo American middle class. The final result of this commitment is that Mexican American culture, language and parentage have been excluded from the classroom. And, the conclusion reached by many as a result of this practice is that Mexican American culture is a hindrance to the student and therefore must be irradicated rather than nourished.

This philosophy has had negative consequences for the child and his parents. Demos (1962) found that Mexican American students hold an unfavorable view of the schools as they are presently constituted. Ramirez (1970) has stated that this cultural exclusion in our schools has another much more devastating effect. It has sharpened the identity problem, so prevalent today among the Mexican American youth. Since his culture is not permitted expression in the classroom, his parents are not able to become active participants in the educational process. This results in a separation of the two worlds in which as a bicultural person he must participate: the world of his parents and the world of the school.

Ramirez further stated that because of this the Mexican American student feels forced to choose between his teachers and his parents, between his Anglo peers and his ethnic peers. This choice causes great turmoil and tension. One can readily understand why Mexican Americans have higher dropout and absenteeism rates. The Mexican American values education and realizes its importance. In order to attain it, however, he must reject his own heritage--a painful process for any human being.

In essence, the "melting pot" philosophy has not only failed in educating, but has also rendered damaging effects in the areas of identity and positive self-concept. Cordasco (1968) appropriately described the implementation of this philosophy as an assault upon an individual in the following words:

> In its effort to assimilate all of its charges; the American school assaulted (and in consequence, very often destroyed) the cultural identity of the child; it forced him to leave his ancestral language at the school house door; it developed in the child a haunting ambivalence of language, of culture, of ethnicity and of personal self-affirmation. It held up to its children mirrors in which they saw not themselves, but the stereotyped middle class, white, English speaking child, who embodied the essence of what the American child was (or ought to be). For the minority child, the images which the school fashioned were cruel deceptions. In the enforced acculturation, there was the rejection of the wellsprings of identity, and more often than not, the failure of achievement.

Negative Attitudes Toward Mexican American Culture

Implicit in the "melting pot" theory is the concept that uniformity is the ideal and that diversity is not acceptable. Fortunately, as the words of Luis Valdez expressed so dramatically in the last section, this concept is changing and diversity is beginning to be looked upon as a positive aspect of American society.

As attitudes toward diversity changed and a need was felt to understand the cultural distinctness of the Mexican American, it fell to the social scientist to provide information on what Mexican American culture entailed. These well-meaning examiners conveniently dichotomized Mexican American and Anglo value systems for this purpose. An example of this type of dichotomy is shown in Figure 1, where Mexican American values are characterized in contrast to corresponding Anglo American values.

The intent of these examiners was to provide information to the teacher concerning the Mexican American culture as a first step in recognizing and respecting the cultural uniqueness of the Mexican American. The opposite result, however, was achieved. The normal interpretation of these dichotomies has been that the Anglo values are regarded as negative. Perhaps one important reason for this unfortunate circumstance is stress placed traditionally on uniformity; that is, anything which is not relative to Anglo American culture is not acceptable.

In essence, the literature which attempts to distinguish Anglo and Mexican American values does not stop with the drawing of a distinction between value orientation. There is always the added suggestion, either implicit or explicit, that traditional Mexican Americans values are dysfunctional and thus need to be changed. The end result has been that these differences have been interpreted as obstacles to the learning process and as something that should be eliminated rather than capitalized upon. Saunders (1954), Edmonson (1957), Madsen (1964), and Zintz (1963), to mention only a few, have all suggested that the chief impediment to academic achievement of the Mexican American is due to the traditional value system of the group. Cecilia Heller's (1965) work is typical of this literature:

> The kind of socialization the Mexican American children receive at home is not conducive to the development of the capacities needed for advancement in a dynamic industrialized society. This type of upbringing creates stumbling blocks to future advancement by stressing values that hinder mobility--family ties, honor, masculinity and living in the present--and by neglecting the values that are conducive to it--achievement, independence and deferred gratification.

Johnson (1971) stated that the Mexican American child owes his primary loyalty to his family, which is likely to have a rigid patriarchal structure. This strong family orientation, in his interpretation, tends to create certain problems in school. According to Johnson:

> Many teachers have complained that Mexican American children exhibit a lack of initiative--they depend on being told explicitly what to do and how to do it. Perhaps this lack of initiative is due to the subordinate role the individual must assume within the Mexican American family structure.

Montiel (1970) in his review of the literature on the Mexican American family has noted that the uncritical use of concepts like "machismo" has relegated all explanation of Mexican family life to a pathological perspective. This perspective views "machismo" as the underlying cause of many problems faced by Mexican Americans and as one of the many traditional cultural traits that this group must overcome if it is to become upwardly mobile.

As essay by Romano (1968) pointed out that the majority of social scientists have concurred in finding the Mexican American to be lacking in history, neurotically passive

Figure 1

TYPICAL CLASSIFICATION OF MAJOR DIFFERENCES BETWEEN
MEXICAN AMERICAN AND ANGLO VALUE SYSTEMS

Mexican American Values	Anglo American Values
Children from traditional Spanish-speaking families may be said to have accepted these general values:	American school teachers are sure to place great value on these practices:
Subjugation to Nature.	Mastery over Nature.
Present Time Orientation.	Future Time Orientation.
Status Based on Ascription.	Status Based on Achievement.
Particularistic Perspective.	Universalistic Perspective.
Emotional.	Affecting Neutral.
Low Level of Aspiration.	High Level of Aspiration.
Work for Present Needs.	Work for Future Success.
Sharing.	Saving.
Nonadherence to Time Schedules.	Adherence to Time Schedules.
Reaction to Change.	Acceptance to Change.
Humility.	Competitive.
Obedience to the Will of God.	Individuality and Self-Realization.
Non-scientific Explanation for Natural Phenomena.	Scientific Explanation for All Behavior.

Source: Adapted from Zintz, Education Across Cultures, 1963.

and fatalistic, lazy and oversexed, criminally prone, superstitious and downright un-American. According to Romano, the conclusion of these examiners is that the Mexican American is stubbornly unwilling to give up his vaguely defined "traditional culture", to forget Spanish, to anglicize his foreign sounding name, become protestant, capitalist, and an unquestioning believer in the American dream.

Andersson and Boyer (1970) reported that Anglos have branded the Mexican American as lazy, clannish, childish and improvident because of his philosophy of life and his value system. These stereotypes have had their repercussions in the classroom, as well as in the larger society, to the point that even many Mexican Americans have come to acknowledge Anglo superiority. One need only look at television, movies, literature, newspapers, and public advertisements, which have for too long inculcated the myth of the lazy, jealous, passive, ignorant and fatalistic Mexican. Such stereotypes have had a steady effect on the unsuspecting viewer, both Anglo and Mexican American alike, from his infancy on. In various ways the public is conditioned to view the Mexican American in a humorous and ridiculous light.

The literature and training produced by our institutions of higher learning have contributed overgeneralized stereotypes and negative images within the minds of many educators. Carter (1970) reaffirmed this when he stated:

> Generalizations have instilled in the minds of most educators a picture of a typical Mexican American and a stereotype of a homogeneous folk culture. The product of this culture is usually seen by educators as a "standard ethnic child," almost predestined to failure in school and ultimately in general society. As one California junior high school principal put it, "The very nature of their culture, their present time orientation, their fatalistic attitudes, being part of the total Latin culture almost prohibits their accepting the long term rewards of the secondary school."

Public school educators, influenced by both the educational literature and popular stereotypes are operating under a subcultural model, which depicts Mexican American life styles as deficient and sees the school as the inculcator of values of the dominant society. In his study of the public school system in the Southwest, Carter (1970) found that:

> The vast majority of educators interviewed for this study and most of the relevant literature argue that Mexican American children are culturally deprived or disadvantaged, that their home environment does not provide the skills, personality characteristics, or experiences necessary for a child's success in school. This view provides most schoolmen with plausible explanation for the failure of Mexican Americans in school.

The sad reality of the matter is that all this studying, analysis and examining has not basically changed the status of the so-called "disadvantaged" Mexican American student, and in many cases it has hurt more than helped. In spite of all the obstacles encountered throughout the educational process, some of these "disadvantaged" students have gone on to obtain graduate degrees and are now critically examining the literature written about them. Romano (1970) suggested that this situation is a unique one in the annals of American social science. It is unique because a population up to now studied is now studying the studiers.

Negative Attitudes Toward Language

Language has been acknowledged by most educational specialists as the major factor which influences the lower achievement levels of the culturally and linguistically different child. There are, however, different schools of thought as to the nature of the language of the minority child and thus differing views on how to deal with that language. Proponents of the "deficit" position advance the theory that the language of the minority child is deficient and that his linguistic capacity in comprehension and productivity in standard English is not as advanced as that of a child from the middle class, mainstream population. Fortunately, the trend today is toward accepting the "difference" theory outlined by Williams (1970) which argues that minority children do have comparably advanced linguistic capacity, but that the language they speak is different in many cases from that of the mainstream population.

Baratz (1970) found that the minority child because of his proficiency in two codes (linguistic systems) is often linguistically advanced as compared to the white middle class child when he enters school. It is only after entering school that the middle class child supercedes the minority child. Baratz further pointed out that it is often the failure of the teacher to recognize that children are speaking a language different from the standard and the consequent negative attitudes toward that language which cause reading problems and the subsequent school failure of the minority child.

The traditional emphasis in the Southwest on language deficiency rather than language differences has made the Mexican American student's experience in school an alien one. From the very first day of school these students have experienced a taste of hostility, beginning with the almost universal rule in the United States against the use of languages other than English in the public schools. The pedagogical arguments for prohibiting Spanish in the Southwest have been:

1. English is the national language and must be learned. The pupil's best interests are served if he speaks English well; English enhances his opportunity for education and employment while Spanish is a handicap.

2. Proper English enables Mexican Americans to compete better with Anglos.

3. Bilingualism is mentally confusing.

4. Southwestern Spanish is a substandard dialect of standard Spanish and therefore unacceptable.

5. Teachers and Anglo pupils do not speak Spanish and it is impolite to speak a language not understood by all.

The suppression of the Spanish language has been the most overt area of exclusion for Mexican Americans. School have repressed languages other than English, regarding them as an educational handicap and a deterrent to Americanization. According to the U.S. Civil Rights Commission Report (1972), 47 percent of the Mexican American first graders in the Southwest do not speak English as well as the average Anglo first grader. These children are often compelled, however, not only to learn a new language, but also to study course material in that language before they have fully mastered it. As Table 10 shows, 30 percent of the elementary schools and 39 percent of the secondary school surveyed in the Southwest admitted discouraging the use of Spanish in the classroom. Methods of enforcing the "no Spanish rule" varied from simple discouragement to strict disciplinary measures.

The suppressive technique of dealing with the language of the "ethnic deviant" has forced the student to believe that his language is inferior to English and that the language learned and spoken at home is somehow evil. This pseudo-concept of language deficiencies rather than language differences implanted in the student a damaging feeling of inferiority which in time has placed a greater learning task on the student.

The importance of Spanish as an educational tool in the acquisition of knowledge by the Mexican American student has not until very recently been fully appreciated nor acknowledged by the Anglo majority. The pioneer in the education of the Spanish-speaking George I. Sanchez (1966), found the persistent belief that a foreign home language is a handicap; that somehow children with Spanish as a mother tongue are doomed to failure--

Table 10

PERCENTAGE OF ELEMENTARY AND SECONDARY SCHOOLS
WHICH DISCOURAGE THE USE OF SPANISH
IN FIVE SOUTHWESTERN STATES

State	Elementary Schools		Secondary Schools	
	Playground	Classroom	Playground	Classroom
Arizona	11.6%	30.4%	11.8%	29.4%
California	4.0%	13.5%	1.8%	18.2%
Colorado	7.8%	15.6%	10.7%	46.4%
New Mexico	7.2%	29.9%	.5%	32.1%
Texas	40.0%	66.4%	34.4%	66.7%
TOTAL SOUTHWEST	15.1%	30.6%	13.9%	39.2%

Source: U.S. Commission on Civil Rights, The Excluded Student, Report III
(May, 1972).

in fact, that they are, by their very nature, less than normally intelligent.
Another educator, Philip D. Ortego (1970), has observed more recently:

> In practice, Mexican American children are frequently relegated to
> classes for the Educable Mentally Retarded simply because many teachers
> equate linguistic ability with intellectual ability. In California,
> Mexican Americans account for more than 40 percent of the so-called
> Mentally Retarded.

The first touchstone of self-identity is a person's name. Yet many teachers have
changed the given names of students for the purpose of obliterating language entities
which were not variables of the dominant language. In so doing, the need for self-
identity was shamefully shunned and neglected. This type of action has forced the
painful process of acculturation which has created psychological problems for many
culturally different students. The desire to be fully accepted by the dominant culture has forced them to alienate themselves from their own, and in so doing, they have
established a low set of values for their own people. Christian (1965) put it well
when he stated:

> It is a personal tragedy and there is much evidence to indicate that it
> is a social tragedy when an adult resents and despises the language or cul-
> ture of his childhood. This may mean that the life he chooses will lack the
> essential meanings which have their roots in infancy; roots which are nour-
> ished by the words his parents have taught him.

36

This resentment creates a paradox within a person leaving him confused and insecure. Sabine Ulibarri (1971) warned against this very clearly when he stated, "We make wonderful truck drivers, lawyers, cement finishers, teachers, but we make lousy gringos."

Andersson and Boyer (1970) stated that the total school experience for the Mexican American has been a very unrealistic one. What was learned at home was not reinforced at school. The language, culture, warmth, plasticity of the home was never found in the school. All of these influences working together have resulted in the destruction of the child's self-image.

Lack of Awareness of the Specialized Needs of the Mexican American Student

Perhaps the lack of awareness of the specialized educational needs of Mexican American students has stemmed in part from the assumption that equal educational opportunity means utilizing the same educational techniques and practices for all students without regard for the differing learning styles and abilities they bring to school. Whatever the reason, this lack of awareness has perpetuated a number of situations which have not been in the best interests of the Mexican American student. Chief among these have been the failure of preservice and inservice programs to provide teachers with the special cultural and linguistic skills necessary for working successfully with Mexican American students; the use of curricula and testing instruments geared to the majority population with little relevance or applicability to the Mexican American students' abilities; the maintenance of schools with the poorest physical facilities in areas where the Mexican American population constitutes the majority; and a general attitude of indifference toward interaction and involvement with the Mexican American community.

Inadequacy of Teachers

Carter's (1970) study disclosed that schools with predominantly Mexican American student populations have traditionally received, and still receive, a disproportionately high percentage of the most poorly trained teachers. The heart of the educational process is, of course, found in the skill, dedication and personality of the teacher. Foremost among the needed qualities of the teacher is respect for the student, which is important in all types of education, at any level, anywhere. With respect for the student, the teacher can become an effective model and inspiration. From this position, the teacher is best able to further the process of learning.

An important factor in the teacher's inability to understand and respect Mexican American students is based on a lack of understanding of a number of general concepts concerning the nature of culture and society and its effects on personality and behavior. Specifically, teachers have not been proficient in three areas:

1. The ability to recognize the influence of culture on personality and behavior.

2. A sufficient knowledge of, or contact with, culturally different groups.

3. An understanding of the role and function of the public school system in general society and especially as an agency of influence on the culturally different student.

Romero's (1966) research on teacher knowledge of the influence of culture on school behavior pointed out the dangers of the casual treatment of culture. Although he found a general awareness of the culture of Mexican American and Anglo students on the part of teachers, he concluded that:

> This teacher awareness . . . could very well be superficial and not based on real knowledge of what constitutes a culture value system. In addition, cultural sensitivity may result from attitudes formed from operating stereotypes. Under this condition a lack of real sensitivity could, in fact, exist.

Ulibarri's (1959) study dealing with teacher awareness and sensitivity to cultural differences found that teachers generally manifest little awareness of the differences among Mexican American, American Indian and Anglo cultures or of the influence each has on children. Most teachers expressed the opinion that school was equally significant and meaningful to children of all groups.

Integrated with a lack of understanding of cultural forces and influences in general is the average teacher's lack of even a superficial knowledge of the specific cultural and linguistic characteristics of the Mexican American people of the Southwest. It is little wonder that Spanish has not been an integral part of instruction when one considers how few teachers in the Southwest actually speak Spanish. As Angel (1968) has so aptly pointed out, even those few teachers who are bilingual do not have the sophisticated skills necessary for developing the instructional strategies necessary for dealing with the complexities of the varying bilingual abilities of individual students. In addition, teacher preparation programs in the past have not provided teachers with resources and information on Mexican American and Hispanic culture which could be incorporated into classroom activities to increase the respect of the Mexican American student for his own cultural heritage.

Inadequacy of Curriculum

Not only is the teacher ill-prepared to deal with the rich bicultural history of the Southwest, but the school curriculum as well has traditionally provided little opportunity for Mexican Americans to learn something about their roots--who they are, where they came from, and what their people have achieved. The curriculum in general and textbooks in particular do not inform either Anglo or Mexican American students of the substantial contributions of the Mexican American culture in the historical development of the Southwest. As Table 11 shows, the third report by the U.S. Commission on Civil Rights (1972) found that of the 1,666 elementary and secondary schools surveyed in the Southwest, only 4.3 percent of the elementary and 7.3 percent of the secondary schools have a course in Mexican American history. This act of ignoring the significance of roles played by Mexican Americans in the development of the United States is simply another facet of cultural exclusion and, needless to say, is not conducive to the development of positive self-image of the student.

The U.S. Commission report further stated that in addition to course content, heritage is also excluded in the cultural selectivity of the schools. School and classroom activity, whenever they deal with Mexican American culture, tend to stress only the superficial and exotic elements, the fantasy heritage of the Southwest. This reinforces existing stereotypes and denies the Mexican American student a full awareness and pride in his culture.

Inadequacy of Testing Instruments

Another obstacle in the education of the Mexican American has been the use of testing instruments which are designed to measure ability and skills typically valued by members of the dominant group. Because of their cultural and linguistic inapplicability to the ability of Mexican American students, these instruments have chastised,

Table 11

PERCENTAGE OF ELEMENTARY AND SECONDARY SCHOOLS
OFFERING MEXICAN AMERICAN HISTORY
IN FIVE SOUTHWESTERN STATES

State	Elementary	Secondary
Arizona	1.5%	11.8%
California	6.6%	9.1%
Colorado	1.3%	10.7%
New Mexico	3.1%	13.3%
Texas	2.1%	1.1%
TOTAL SOUTHWEST	4.3%	7.3%

Source: U.S. Commission on Civil Rights, The Excluded Student, REport III (May, 1972).

ridiculed and convinced culturally different students and their teachers that they are inferior and predestined to lower accomplishments. Yourman (1964) substantiated this when he stated:

> Cultural and personality differences do affect group intelligence scores to the extent that they become low in predictive validity when used for cross-cultural capacity of capacity to learn; and the labeling of a child with a "permanent" stratification index (I.Q.) is likely to affect his self-concept, his goals, his motivations and achievements.

Before the student gets too far in school, I.Q. tests have seriously harmed him. Carter (1970) considers these tests to be merely measures of learned items of culture, not indicators of intellectual potentiality or capacity. An I.Q. test tends to measure how much "average culture" has been internalized and can be elicited by the proper stimulua--that is the degree of acculturation of individual enculturation. The use of these instruments has resulted in the misplacement of countless Mexican American students in the lowest educational tracks. According to Carter:

> The failure of standard psychometric instruments to measure Mexican American children validly is recognized as a principal reason for the over-representation of that ethnic group in Special Education, as well as other low tracks.

One important factor which affects the performance of Mexican American children on standardized tests is that of language. Ortego (1970) has pointed out that many Mexican Americans are considered to be mentally retarded because their linguistic ability in standard English is not sufficient for them to perform adequately on standardized tests.

An important variable in the use of standardized test instruments is the role of the test interpreter. As an example, Carter (1970) cited the experience of two psychologists, one Anglo and one Spanish-speaking. Using standard instruments, they were testing to see which children should be placed in Special Education classes. The Anglo examiner recommended that 75 percent of these Mexican American children be placed in these classes, whereas the Spanish-speaking examiner recommended that only 26 percent of these children be placed in these classes. Such decisions indicate that the importance of the test interpreter as a variable in the evaluation process should receive more attention.

Inadequacy of School Facilities

Poor facilities have always affected the quality of education. Surveys of the 1930's indicated that the physical facilities in predominantly Mexican American schools were run down, badly maintained, overcrowded, poorly furnished and lacking in equipment. Although these conditions are no longer universal, they are still encountered. Carter (1970) stated that in many sections of the Southwest the contrast between the physical facilities of predominantly minority group schools and middle class institutions is immense.

The second report by the U.S. Commission on Civil Rights (1971) reported that Mexican Americans have been severely isolated by school districts and by individual schools within certain districts. This obviously indicates one thing--gerrymandering to accomplish the separate but unequal school conditions that have been traditional in American history. According to the Commission's report, this situation still exists throughout the Southwest.

Indifference to the Needs of the Mexican American Community

Historically, there has been an indifference on the part of the schools to relate with the Mexican American community. To determine the extent of community involvement in southwestern schools, the third report of the U.S. Commission on Civil Rights (1972) examined the nature of these schools; contact with parents, and the extent of their reliance on the use of community advisory boards, community relations specialists and consultants on Mexican American education.

Teachers and administrators utilize notices sent home and P.T.A. meetings most frequently as methods of communicating with parents. Although over four million persons in the Southwest identify Spanish as their mother tongue, the Commission report discovered that only 25 percent of the elementary schools and 11 percent of the secondary schools send notices in Spanish to Spanish-speaking parents. The report also stated that in the schools of the Southwest 91.7 percent of the elementary and 98.5 percent of the secondary do not use Spanish as well as English in conducting P.T.A. meetings.

Contacts with parents and community advisory boards are methods by which schools can communicate directly with Mexican American parents and the community in general. However, according to the report, only one district in four actually has a community advisory board on Mexican American educational affairs. When these methods prove unsuccessful in the establishment of free communication, a community relations specialist may be called in to serve as a link between the people and the power structure. The report demonstrated that 84 percent of the surveyed districts did not use community relations specialists at all. Thus, in spite of the need, most school systems have not established this type of liaison with the community.

The report further stated that the data concerning the use of Mexican American educational consultants is similar. School districts are not availing themselves of experts who could help them to determine and to resolve their failures in educating the Mexican American student.

CHAPTER IV

A CURRENT PERSPECTIVE ON BILINGUAL-BICULTURAL
EDUCATION AND TEACHER PREPARATION PROGRAMS

With the educational plight of the Mexican American student viewed in perspective and with some insight into the apparent causes of his deficient educational accomplishment, it is appropriate and imperative to explore a possible solution to this problem--bilingual-bicultural education. In so doing, a rationale for bilingual-bicultural education in general will be formulated which describes its advantages to both minority group children and the population as a whole. Additionally, and more specific to the nature of this study, a rationale will be formulated for the maintenance of bilingual-bicultural education programs in secondary schools.

In an effort to bring to light exactly what is meant by bilingual-bicultural education, an examination will be made of the nature of bilingual-bicultural education as it exists today. Since the success of any educational program is dependent on the expertise of the teachers directing it in the classroom, and since a major goal of this study is to define what determines the expertise of a bilingual-bicultural education teacher, this chapter will conclude with an examination of the present status of bilingual-bicultural teacher preparation programs in the United States.

Rationale for Bilingual-Bicultural Education

Andersson and Boyer (1970) have summarized a rationale for bilingual-bicultural schooling in the United States in the following propositions:

1. American schooling has not met the needs of children coming from homes where non-English languages are spoken. A radical improvement is therefore urgently needed.

2. Such improvement must first of all maintain and strengthen the sense of identity of children entering the schools from such homes.

3. The self-image and sense of dignity of families that speak other languages must also be preserved and strengthened.

4. The child's mother tongue is not only an essential part of his self-identity; it is also his best instrument for learning, especially in the early stages.

5. Preliminary evidence indicates that initial learning through a child's non-English home language does not hinder learning in English or other school subjects.

6. Differences among first, second and foreign languages need to be understood if learning through them is to be sequenced effectively.

7. The best order of the learning of basic skills in a language--whether first or second--needs to be understood and respected if best results are to be obtained. This order is normally, especially for children: listening, comprehension, speaking, reading and writing.

8. Young children have an impressive learning capacity, especially in the case of language learning. The young child learns more easily and better than adolescents or adults in adopting the sound system, the basic structure, and vocabulary of a language.

9. Closely related to bilingualism is biculturalism, which should be an integral part of bilingual instruction.

10. Bilingual education holds the promise of helping to harmonize various ethnic elements in a community into a mutually respected and creative pluralistic society.

While the preceding rationale contains many viable reasons to support the value of bilingual education, perhaps the most influential argument for bilingual education is seen in point number 4, which states that, "The child's mother tongue . . is . . his best instrument for learning, especially in the early stages." In order to stress this particular point, Andersson and Boyer (1970) presented a portion of Gaarder's statement to Senator Yarborough's Special Subcommittee on Bilingual Education, in which Gaarder emphasized:

Children who enter school with less competence in English than mono-lingual English-speaking children will probably become retarded in their school work to the extent of their deficiency in English, if English is the sole medium of instruction. On the other hand, the bilingual child's conceptual development and acquisition of other experiences and information could proceed at a normal rate if the mother tongue were used as an alternate medium of instruction.

There is a growing body of research which substantiates conclusively Gaarder's assertion that the use of the mother tongue in instruction can enable bilingual or bidialectal children to progress at a normal rate. Indeed, there is evidence to prove that children progress more rapidly if the mother tongue is used as the first language of instruction.

Modiano (1968) stated that in Chiapas, Mexico an experimental group of children was taught to read in their native Indian dialect. When the children had mastered their Indian primers, they entered first grade where all subsequent instruction was carried out in the national language, Spanish. Test results showed that those Indian children who had first been taught to read in their native language read Spanish better and with greater comprehension than those children who had received instruction only in Spanish.

According to John (1969), another bilingual experiment in Sweden produced similar results. A group of children received an initial ten weeks of reading instruction in their local dialect. They were then switched to instruction in literary Swedish. By the end of the first year, the experimental group had surpassed the control group in all language art skills in literary Swedish.

Experiments by researchers in multilingual nations all over the world--Orata (1953) in the Phillipines, McNamara (1966) in Ireland, Pena (1970) in Texas, and Malherbe (1946) in South Africa, to cite only a few--have shown that children who have been taught to read in their home language first, become better readers in the language of the school than control groups who do not have the advantage of using the home language first.

Another important reason for bilingual education for culturally and linguistically different children, cited in Andersson and Boyer's rationale, is the need to link home and school experiences as an important factor in reinforcing self-identity. In order to stress this particular need, they quote two further points from Gaarder's statement to the Special Subcommittee on Bilingual Education:

1.   Non-English-speaking children come from non-English-speaking homes.
     The use of the child's mother tongue by some teacher and as a
     school language is necessary if there is to be a strong, mutually
     reinforcing relationship between the home and the school.

2.   Language is the most important exteriorization or manifestation
     of the self and human personality. If the all-powerful schools
     reject the mother tongue of an entire group of children, it can
     be expected to seriously and adversely affect these children's
     concept of their parents, their homes and themselves.

     As is the case with Andersson and Boyer's rationale for bilingual education,
most such rationale stress only those aspects of bilingual education which are beneficial for the culturally and linguistically different child. There is, however, a
growing body of literature which argues very persuasively that achieving bilingualism
can be of great benefit to all children. A study by Lambert and Peal (1962) of
French and English-speaking bilinguals in Montreal revealed that if bilingualism were
"balanced"--that is, if there had been some equal, normal literacy development in two
languages--bilingual 19-year-olds in Montreal were markedly superior to monolinguals
on verbal and non-verbal tests of intelligence. In addition, these "balanced" bilinguals appeared to have greater mental flexicility, superior concept formation and a
more advanced set of mental attitudes.
     The documentation presented on the affect of bilingual education on both monolin-
gual and bilingual children is conclusively in favor of bilingual education. However,
bilingual education cannot be truly effective when separated from bicultural education.
According to Jaramillo (1972):

     It is time that we all understand, if we do not already, that bilingual
     education without consideration of the cultural component is obsolete. It
     can be argued successfully that knowledge of two or more languages is an
     asset to intellectual development. Certainly bilingualism assists one's
     power of perception by giving one access to two or more languages and in that
     way substantially increases the number of ideas to which one has access. But
     the additional tools for perception to which a bilingual person has access
     are not nearly as powerful as those of a person who is not only bilingual but
     bicultural as well.

While Andersson and Boyer's rationale stresses primarily bilingual education, it
does make reference to the need to incorporate bicultural aspects into a bilingual program. Jaramillo (1972), however, has offered a concrete argument for the advantages
biculturalism can offer to the nation as a whole. In the following statement, she has
outlined how biculturalism can lead to an increased tolerance through the ability to
view behavior and experiences in terms of differing points of view rather than as
right and wrong:

     The benefit to intellectual development of the bicultural person is
     more than having access to two cultural points of view. In many situations
     a bicultural person will find that the attitudes of the two cultures in
     which he lives truly conflict. If he is truly bicultural, he realizes it
     will not be because one attitude is true and one is false, or that one
     attitude is good and one is bad, but that the conflict is simply one of
     attitudes and not of truths. He will think of appropriateness and avail-
     able stock of behaviors from which to pick and choose. From this he begins
     to understand the concept of point of view. He learns that a point of view
     does not express a truth but simply an attitude, a way to look at the world.
     This is one of the major advantages of biculturalism.

Clearly, the development of bicultural persons as Jaramillo has described will lead to a decrease of cultural conflict in American society. This writer's own interpretation is that the development of such awareness will result in the erradication of the stereotypes outlined in Chapter III, which have been so damaging to the self-concept of members of all minority groups. Only through this kind of sensitivity will it be possible to interpret the social scientists' dichotomies of cultural values in terms of positive differences, each having particular value and appropriateness in relation to specific situations and conditions, rather than in terms of equating all Anglo values with good qualities and all Mexican American values with bad qualities.

While Jaramillo's statement of the benefits of biculturalism are directed at the total population of the United States, the incorporation of the cultural component in bilingual-bicultural education has special significance for minority groups. Both Ramirez (1970) and Cordasco (1968) have implied in their condemnation of the educational system for its lack of cultural relevance to the Mexican American student, that the incorporation of the cultural component will have a tremendous impact on the educational success of Mexican American students. By reinforcing home culture, there will be a reduction in the conflict, which exists now according to Ramirez, between the Mexican American student's home and school experiences--a conflict which has often driven him away from school.

Rationale for Maintenance of Bilingual-Bicultural Programs on the Secondary Level

Bilingual-bicultural education should not be looked upon as a tool for assimilation, as another form of compensatory education, or as merely a bridge to learning the national language and culture. Likewise, the development of bilingual-bicultural skills should not be considered a process that must be terminated at a specific grade level. Instead, both should be viewed as a continuing social force that must be nourished to sophisticated level if we are to expect our students to become truly bilingual-bicultural individuals--functional in and appreciative of two cultures and languages.

The concept of bilingualism-biculturalism is beginning to be considered a positive identity factor not only for improved self-concept for minority students, but, as Jaramillo (1972) has pointed out, the mark of a broader education with a wider societal perspective. Minority groups are demonstrating a desire to have their languages and cultures become integral components of the total school curriculum, not only in grades one to twelve, but also on the college level.

Gaarder (as quoted in Andersson and Boyer, 1970) has provided two reasons which support the maintenance of bilingual-bicultural education programs on the secondary level and above:

1. If he has not achieved reasonable literacy in his mother tongue (ability to read, write and speak accurately) it will be virtually useless to him for any technical or professional work where language matters. Thus his unique potential career advantage, his bilingualism, will have been destroyed.

2. Our people's native competence in Spanish, French, Czech and all other languages with the cultural heritage each language transmits are a national resource that we need badly and must conserve by every reasonable means.

Ornstein (1974) has also pointed out that sophisticated bilingual skills in reading and writing as well as in oral communication are essential in today's advanced technological society. One or two foreign language courses at the secondary level are insufficient for most students to achieve this level of sophistication. From research carried out at the Cross-Cultural Southwest Ethnic Study Center at the University of success by Mexican American students, revealed that one of the most damaging patterns today is the inability of the educational system to hold minority students in school past the eighth grade. According to the U.S. Civil Rights Commission Report V (1973), the fault does not lie with these students but with the educational process itself:

> It is the schools and teachers of the Southwest, not the children, who are failing. They are failing in meeting their most basic responsibility-- that of providing each child the opportunity to gain the maximum benefit of education and develop his capabilities to the fullest extent. In the Commission's view, the schools of the Southwest will continue to fail until fundamental changes are made. Changes are needed in the way teachers are trained and in the standards by which they are judged, and changes are needed in educational programs and curriculums so that all children are reached.

In this writer's opinion, bilingual-bicultural education is the humane approach to meeting the long neglected needs of the Mexican American student. His bilingualism and biculturalism have for too long been considered a problem, when in fact as Jaramillo (1972) has pointed out, they are really his most valuable asset. Developed to the level of English language and cultural skills, they can be a powerful tool and his special advantage for access to upward social and economic mobility.

The Nature of Bilingual-Bicultural Education

Bilingual-bicultural education is not a new concept in education. According to Lewis (1973) it has existed throughout the world in one form or another since ancient time. Among the countries that have accepted this educational practice in their public schools as a matter of general policy are Belgium, France, Finland, Canada, Yugoslavia and the Soviet Union.

In the United States bilingual schooling has existed since non-English-speaking immigrants first set foot on American soil. Andersson and Boyer (1970) have traced bilingual education in the United States from 1839 (German in Minnesota, French in Louisiana, and Spanish in New Mexico were used as mediums of instruction.) to the rebirth of bilingual education in 1963 in Miami. The Dade County Florida Schools, in an attempt to meet the educational needs of Cuban children who were coming into the public schools, established a completely bilingual program in grades one, two and three. This effort to provide for the needs of the Spanish-speaking children sparked the initiation of other bilingual programs throughout the United States. The impetus of this program, as cited in the Guide to Title VII Programs (1972-1973), was such that, currently, bilingual education projects are conducted in 29 states of the United States, Guam, the Mariana Islands, Puerto Rico and the Virgin Islands. These projects represent 24 languages and dialects including English.

Bilingual-bicultural education has been defined in a variety of ways. Of the many diverse definitions, perhaps the most adequate one in encompassing the essence of bilingual-bicultural education is contained in the Manual for Project Applicants and Grantees (1972) for programs under the Bilingual Education Act:

> Bilingual education is the use of two languages, one of which is English, as mediums of instruction for the same pupil population in a well organized program which encompasses part of all of the curriculum and includes the study of the history and culture associated with the mother tongue. A complete program develops and maintains the children's self-esteem and a legitimate pride in both cultures.

Bilingual-bicultural education in the United States historically has been concentrated in the lower grades, usually terminating somewhere between grades four and six.

And, although the definition above for bilingual programs includes the study of history and culture, the major emphasis in fact has been on language to the exclusion of the cultural component. The use of the native tongue has served mainly as a bridge to learning the national language. Mackey (1970) described such a curriculum as the Transfer type. He noted that:

> The Transfer Model has been used to convert from one medium to another
> . . . In schools of this type, the transfer may be gradual or abrupt, regular
> or irregular, the degree of regularity and gradualness being available as to
> distinguish one school from another.

Under this type of model, after four to six years of bilingual education, the student is expected to function as an English monolingual, with only occasional and random attention to any residual language problem he might still retain. Often, in the view of the U.S. Civil Rights Commission Report III (1972), the study of culture is superficial and based on a "fantasy" approach with little relevance to the student's real historical and cultural heritage. The result of such an approach is in essence no more than another aspect of cultural exclusion. As the report stated:

> The fantasy heritage idealized life in the Far West as a gay pageant
> of leisurely pleasures, guided by kindly mission padres and rich benevolent
> ranchers (all with Spanish pedigrees) whose generosity, paternal love, and
> regularly scheduled fiestas endeared them to the humble, somewhat shift-
> less Indians and Mexicans who tended their crops and rounded up their cattle.
> The "fantasy heritage" exemplifies cultural selectivity in action. It
> embraces the mythical charm of early California: Spanish food, Spanish music,
> Spanish costumes, the rancheros, caballeros and senoritas with gardenias be-
> hind their ears. The main trouble with this view of Mexican American life
> is that it bears no relation to reality, past or present.

In many places, bilingual programs in the elementary schools have been little more than compensatory or remedial language programs in disguise. Although these programs have utilized the children's home language in school, the U.S. Civil Rights Commission Report III (1972) has pointed out that this was done mainly to facilitate the learning of English and excluded the cultural component. Sometimes the programs have simply been another approach to hasten the process of assimilation and remove the "foreign-ness" or "Mexicanness" of the children.

One thing that experience has taught, as bilingual-bicultural education pro-gresses, is that no one particular model is applicable to every geographic area. The Mexican American student in New Mexico is unique, and thus his needs are unique, in relation to the Mexican American student from the Midwest or other southwestern states. Linguistic ability and cultural experiences vary among Mexican Americans depending upon recency of family migration, proximity to the United States-Mexican border and income level. Low income families are less able to afford homes in assimilated middle class communities in the cities and suburban areas where English is used with greater frequency and fluency by Mexican Americans.

According to Pascual (1973) the selection and consideration of any bilingual-bicultural model should be based on a determination of the specific needs and require-ments of the particular school in question. Some of the basic issues which must be established before selection of a model is decided are:

1. The overall purpose and goals of the program as determined by the educational needs of the students, the general needs of the com-munity, and state and local public school requirements.

2. The nature of the student population to be served; ethnic composi-tion; language abilities in English and Spanish; needs and priorities of the students.

3. The type of instructional strategies that will be most effective; separate or mixed language instruction; use of standard or regional Spanish or both; division of English and Spanish components; emphasis on culture and history and fine arts.

4. The competencies and skills needed by teachers to implement the program in relation to the expertise of the faculty on hand.

These issues and many more which are affected by the environment of the community, the school or school system, and by polities and standards set forth by the State Department of Education should be considered before implementing a bilingual-bicultural program in any school on any level.

Since the educational needs of the Mexican American are the prime focus of most bilingual-bicultural programs, issues which determine the selection of a model will be based on the best interests of these students. However, it is important to emphasize that in acknowledging the multilingual-multicultural character of our nation, it is imperative that the native English-speaking student also be benefited from such a program. Only then will the positive effects of bilingual-bicultural education be completely realized and acknowledged.

Pascual (1973) has presented a plan for a bilingual-bicultural curriculum which can be easily implemented in the junior and senior high school. The models depicted in Figure 2 are designed to illustrate Pascual's plan.

The junior high model refers to a plan in which the general requirements are presented in English. A Spanish Language Arts class is a daily part of the curriculum for all students who have developed basic skills in Spanish in grades 1-6. Composition, language analysis and literature are emphasized. Another integral component of the curriculum is an English-Spanish Fine Arts class that provides instruction in both cultures. Students are exposed to fine arts (Anglo-Saxon content) in English three days a week, and fine arts (Hispanic content) in Spanish two days a week. Foreign language classes, per se, are not offered since the student is functioning already in two languages.

The high school model presents a plan in which Spanish Language Arts, Social Studies and English as a Second Language are combined in one block. The model also provides for the teaching of elective courses such as Fine Arts, Literature, World History, Spanish as a Second Language, Business Education or any other elective which would maintain and expand the concepts of bilingualism-biculturalism for those wishing to remain in the bilingual curriculum. These courses are taught in Spanish. The other general high school requirements are presented in English.

Because of the nature of the secondary curriculum and the personal decisions to be made by the student, the secondary curriculum in Spanish should be elective in nature. Pascual (1973) has emphasized that Spanish-speaking students should not be placed in classes where Spanish is taught as a foreign language. Instead, they should be placed in a Spanish class where instruction follows a language arts approach.

The models illustrated in Figure 2 and described above serve to give a picture of the type of bilingual-bicultural programs which can be and are being implemented in the United States today. As a further explanation of how bilingual-bicultural education functions, Appendix A provides a brief description of 21 bilingual-bicultural programs which are specifically designed for Mexican American students on the secondary level and which are currently in operation. These 21 programs were isolated from a list of a total of 216 bilingual-bicultural projects in the United States identified by the Dissimination Center for Bilingual-Bicultural Education (1972-1973).

An examination of these secondary programs described in Appendix A reveals that their major stress is on English and Spanish language arts, emphasizing proficiency in both languages. The core curriculum of some of the programs is taught bilingually are social studies, science and math.

In an attempt to improve the self-concept and cultural pride of the student, courses have been included to provide instruction in folk singing and art; Hispanic,

Figure 2

A MODEL FOR SCHEDULING BILINGUAL-BICULTURAL EDUCATION
PROGRAMS IN JUNIOR AND SENIOR HIGH SCHOOL

Grades 7-8

	Monday	Tuesday	Wednesday	Thursday	Friday
Classroom Periods			General		
			Junior		
			High School		
			Requirements		
	////	////	Spanish Language Arts ////	////	////
		////	English and Spanish Fine Arts ////	////	

Grades 9-12

	Monday	Tuesday	Wednesday	Thursday	Friday
Classroom Periods	////	////	Spanish Language Arts ////	////	////
	////	////	Social Studies ////	////	////
			English as a Second Language		
			Electives		
			Other General		
			High School Requirements		

*Shaded areas denote instruction in Spanish; unshaded areas denote instruction in English.

Source: Adapted from Pascual, "Bilingual Education for New Mexico's Schools", 1973.

Mexican and Southwest culture; and Southwest literature.

English as a Second Language instruction has been included in three programs in order to serve students with very limited English ability and also to allow students to experience a different English language learning experience.

Community involvement is encouraged in some programs through the use of home visitation, parent advisory councils, and other techniques to solicit parent-community participation.

It is imperative to emphasize again that conditions and needs relative to a particular locale should be given due consideration in ascertaining the type of bilingual-bicultural program that will be effective for each geographic area. It is in this way alone that bilingual-bicultural curricula can have relevancy and applicability in meeting the differing needs of the Mexican American students in our country. Hopefully, as a consequence, these students will be able to overcome the economic and social inequities which they have suffered from previous educational experiences.

Present Status of Bilingual-Bicultural
Teacher Preparation Programs

A perspective on bilingual-bicultural education in the United States today is not complete without a look at the training available for the teachers who are most directly responsible for carrying out these programs. There is ample evidence that traditional teacher preparation is not sufficient to provide teachers with the special skills need to work with culturally and linguistically different children. Angel (1968), Aragon (1971), Carter (1970), Valencia (1972), and Manuel (1968), to name only a few, have all acknowledged the lack of and the crucial need for special preparation for teachers who will work in bilingual-bicultural programs.

In order to determine the extent of bilingual-bicultural teacher training programs in the United States today, a nation wide survey was conducted by this author during the fall of 1973. The first step of the survey was to identify those states having a State Program Director for Bilingual Education and those states having special certification requirements for bilingual-bicultural teachers. (See Appendix B for letter sent out.) With this information existing university and college programs designed for the preparation of teachers in bilingual-bicultural education programs could be identified.

With a 100 percent response to the initial letter, it was determined that the following states have a person designated as the State Program Director for Bilingual Education who is not a foreign language consultant: Alaska, Arizona, California, Connecticut, Illinois, Indiana, Massachusetts, Michigan, New Jersey, New Mexico and Texas. Several states have a person designated as consultant, specialist, supervisor or coordinator for bilingual programs. These states are: Colorado, Iowa, Louisana, Maine, Maryland, Montana, New York, Rhode Island, and Washington. States reporting special certification or some type of criteria for teachers in bilingual schools are: Arizona, California, Maine, Massachusetts, New Mexico, Texas and Wisconsin.

A number of institutions in several states were identified as having programs currently underway in the preparation of teachers for bilingual-bicultural education programs. Only those institutions, however, which revealed a certain level of sophistication in preparing teachers for bilingual-bicultural programs, are included in Table 12. The level of sophistication was determined by examining the rationale for the program, the course content and the nature of the field experience offered to the student. A brief description of the content, focus and depth of these programs is included in Appendix C.

Of the 19 institutions included in the table, 16 listed language as a required discipline. The program descriptions were not specific in regard to prerequisite language skills. Statements included were, for example, language mastery; competence in English and a foreign language; satisfactory degree of proficiency and a knowledge and understanding of Spanish spoken in Mexico and the Southwest. Ten institutions did not specify prerequisite language skills. The implication appears to be that candidates selecting the bilingual-bicultural preparation curriculum would be native speakers of Spanish and therefore have the necessary oral-aural skills.

The institutions which did indicate language skills as a prerequisite were not clear concerning the evaluation of language skills. Five institutions made no provision for evaluation, and the five that did, used oral exams, advisor judgement, foreign language department judgement, or a placement test. Descriptions of the tests were not available.

Strong emphasis was given to Educational Foundations courses and methods courses dealing with the education of the Spanish-speaking student. The areas of culture, history and sociocultural awareness were given strong priority. Other courses offered relating to the Spanish-speaking culture were psychology, philosophy, anthropology, political science, fine arts and TESOL methodology.

The two areas given the least priority were actual application of the skills acquired and school-community relations. It is interesting to note, especially in view of the purpose of this study, that all of the programs provided instruction for teachers who would work on the elementary level. None of the programs were designed for teachers who would work on the secondary level. On the basis of this information the need for teacher preparation programs in bilingual-bicultural education for the secondary level is obvious.

CHAPTER V

IDENTIFICATION OF THE SPECIAL COMPETENCIES NEEDED
BY TEACHERS IN BILINGUAL-BICULTURAL
EDUCATION PROGRAMS

As a preliminary step in determining the priorities of a bilingual-bicultural teacher preparation program, this study has outlined a profile of the Mexican American student and examined some of the apparent past causes of his underachievement. In addition to considering the needs of the students in bilingual-bicultural education programs, however, the development of the teacher training related to these programs should also rely on the concerns and needs expressed by those persons who participate in the direction and formation of these programs. In order to ascertain the priorities of educational administrators, researchers, practicing teachers, teacher trainees, Mexican American interest groups and community members, the following strategies were utilized:

1. An extensive survey of current educational literature regarding bilingual-bicultural teacher preparation was made.

2. During 1973 the writer attended a number of bilingual-bicultural education related conferences including: the Chicano Mobile Institute in Albuquerque; the New Mexico Bilingual TESOL Conference in Las Vegas, New Mexico; the National TESOL Convention in San Juan, Puerto Rico; the National Bilingual-Bicultural Institute in Albuquerque; and the Bilingual/Cross-Cultural Specialist Credential Conference in San Diego, California. These conferences were attended by educational researchers, administrators, teacher trainers, teachers and university students. The consensus of conference participants regarding priorities for teacher education was examined in detail.

3. The survey of existing university teacher preparation programs in bilingual-bicultural education described in the preceding chapter and outlined in Appendix C revealed its priorities through an examination of course content and emphasis.

4. Information made available from the Institute for Cultural Pluralism at San Diego State University provided opinions from a number of interest groups. During the fall of 1973, the Institute solicited information from university students, teachers, teacher trainers, ethnic studies departments, community members and educational administrators in the San Diego area regarding their priorities for competencies for teachers in bilingual/cross-cultural classrooms. This information was thoroughly analyzed. (A copy of the cover letter and questionnaire circulated by the Institute appears in Appendix D.)

One of the initial results of these investigations was the identification of four broad areas of expertise which were considered essential for prospective teachers in bilingual-bicultural education programs. These areas are: language, culture, professional education, and school-community relations. Following a format which will examine each of these areas in detail, this chapter will outline the specific competencies identified by each of the four studies described above as they relate to

52

language, culture, professional education and school-community relations.

Language

The literature referred frequently to the importance of using the student's home language in school, both as a medium of communication in the school environment and as a medium of instruction. The specific criteria of the language competence required by teachers, however, was at times vague and varied from author to author. Sanchez (1970) stated:

> We need to produce more bilingual teachers. How can you have bilingual education if you don't have bilingual teachers? It is true, of course, that in some places where they are operating bilingual programs, they do have bilingual teachers. In others they are making up for the monolingualism of the English-speaking teacher by having some one who speaks Spanish come in and teach that part of the curriculum in Spanish. It is a good device, but a better one is to produce teachers who are truly bilingual, not simply teachers who know Spanish.

Smith (1968), an advocate of ESL programs for Mexican Americans, did not consider it compulsory for the teacher to be fluent in Spanish. She did recognize, however, that some knowledge of the language would be an asset in enabling the teacher to establish a rapport with the students and serving as a bridge for clarifying concepts and making explanations.

Kayser (1969) interpreted language competence for teachers as a thorough familiarity with the structures of the Spanish and English language and the ability to select and construct materials for the teaching of subject matter in those languages. The teacher, he felt, must be able to teach habits of articulation effectively in order to avoid and overcome interference of the speech habits of one language or the other.

Gaarder's (1965) opinion of teacher competence in language supported the dual language, dual literacy aims of many bilingual programs. He believed that, for a successful bilingual program, teachers of English should be native speakers or have near native proficiency in order to meet the vernacular needs of the students.

Jaramillo (1973) felt that teachers must study both English and Spanish in depth and that all courses in the general studies area should be available in both languages. The language to be used should be determined by the content of the course. She felt that certain courses, such as Southwest History, Mexican Art, and Spanish literature, lend themselves to study in Spanish.

Carter (1969) felt that perhaps the biggest skill failing among teachers of Mexican American students was the almost universal inability to communicate in Spanish. He concluded that all factions seem to concur that this skill is essential for teachers of this minority group. Furthermore, he stated that there is no valid reason, except institutional ineptitude and rigidity, why teachers should not become relatively proficient in a language spoken by so many of their students.

Concerning language competence for teachers, Samora (1966) felt:

> To qualify, the teacher of Spanish-speaking children should be an unquestionably good teacher. It would help for such a good teacher to know Spanish (to have casual conversation with the child, to talk with the parents, to appreciate the problems and virtues of bilingualism), but the important thing is that she be a good teacher and that she be given an opportunity to do her job (reasonable class size, at least average help from her superiors, and the like). If the teacher does not know Spanish she should at least understand why some of her Spanish-speaking pupils have particular difficulties.

Participants at the bilingual-bicultural education related conferences supported the need for bilingual language competence for teachers in bilingual-bicultural programs. It was felt that merely being bilingual did not necessarily mean that a teacher had knowledge or could exhibit teaching skills in a bilingual instructional program. The linguistic competencies considered essential and fundamental for a bilingual teacher covered a broad spectrum of skills, knowledge and attitudes including the following:

1. A knowledge of the student's home dialect.

2. An ability to communicate in Spanish on a second level-- that of classroom commands and directions.

3. An ability to communicate at the instructional level.

4. An ability to communicate at a professional level.

5. The ability to predict and understand student's language problems due to interference between the two languages.

6. The general ability to speak, read, and write Spanish with grammatical accuracy and style.

It was the general consensus of the conference participants that inservice training programs were needed in schools targeted for bilingual instruction if teachers who were especially trained for bilingual-bicultural education programs were not available. The participants felt that graduates from the usual secondary education programs lacked the skills to execute effectively the teaching of content in Spanish.

The latest report of the U.S. Commission on Civil Rights (1974) stated that in their review of college catalogues from 25 randomly selected Southwestern institutions, they found that not one school of education had a stated policy requiring teacher trainees to take Spanish as part of their liberal arts course work or to be conversant with the language.

At the National Bilingual Bicultural Institute, cosponsored by the National Education Task Force de la Raza and the National Education Association and held on November 28 through December 1, 1973 in Albuquerque, New Mexico, a survey was conducted to determine priorities in the preparation of teachers for bilingual-bicultural education programs. Participants were asked to rate on a one-to-five scale the degree of priority they placed on a number of specific teacher competencies. One indicated highest priority on the scale, and five indicated lowest priority. One sample item from the survey instrument is shown below:

<table>
<tr><td></td><td>High</td><td></td><td></td><td>Low</td></tr>
<tr><td>Priority that the teacher be bilingual:</td><td>1 2</td><td>3</td><td>4</td><td>5</td></tr>
</table>

Table 12 illustrates the degree of priority which the respondents gave to three specific competencies: Bilingual Ability, Knowledge of Children's Cultural Environment, and Knowledge of Bilingual-Bicultural Teaching Strategies. The absolute number of respondents to each value from one to five is given for each competency along with the percentage figure this absolute number reflects.

There were approximately 1,300 participants at the Institute of which 679 formally registered. According to computer listings, the Institute attracted participants from 25 states and Mexico. The majority of the registered participants came from five states and Washington, D.C. These included 240 participants from New Mexico; 94 from Colorado; 92 from Texas; 75 from California; 33 from Arizona; and 46 from Washington, D.C. Other states represented at the Institute were Florida, Georgia, Idaho, Indiana, Illinois, Kansas, Maryland, Massachusetts, Michigan, Minnesota, New York, Nebraska, Nevada, Ohio, Oregon, Tennessee, Utah, Virginia, Washington, and Wisconsin.

Table 12

DEGREE OF PRIORITY GIVEN TO BILINGUAL ABILITY, KNOWLEDGE OF CHILDREN'S CULTURAL ENVIRONMENT, AND KNOWLEDGE OF BILINGUAL-BICULTURAL TEACHING STRATEGIES AS COMPETENCIES FOR BILINGUAL-BICULTURAL TEACHER TRAINEES BY EDUCATORS AT THE NATIONAL BILINGUAL BICULTURAL INSTITUTE (1973)

C O M P E T E N C I E S

Value Label	Value	Bilingual Ability		Knowledge of Children's Cultural Environment		Knowledge of Bilin.-Bicul. Teaching Strategies	
		Number Responding	Percentage Responding	Number Responding	Percentage Responding	Number Responding	Percentage Responding
No Response	0.0	3	1.4%	6	2.7%	10	4.5%
High Priority	1.0	168	76.4%	203	92.3%	149	67.7%
	2.0	31	14.1%	6	2.7%	38	17.3%
	3.0	13	5.9%	2	0.9%	13	5.9%
	4.0	2	0.9%	0	–	7	3.2%
Low Priority	5.0	3	1.4%	3	1.4%	3	1.4%
TOTALS		220	100.0%	220	100.0%	220	100.0%

Source: The National Task Force de la Raza, An Evaluation of the National Bilingual-Bicultural Institute, 1973.

55

In measuring the degree of priority placed on bilingualism as a competence necessary for teachers training for bilingual-bicultural education programs, the Institute survey revealed that a high percentage (90.5 percent) of the respondents gave bilingualism a high priority (see Table 12). In view of the fact that there were some 220 respondents in the survey, representing the views of administrators, project coordinators, teachers, university professors, community members and students, these findings take on great significance. More important is the fact that these participants came from a total of 25 states in this country and thus represent a wide variety of regional interests. These findings can help set new trends in bilingual-bicultural teacher preparation.

The survey of the existing university programs offering courses for the preparation of teachers for bilingual-bicultural programs identified language competence as:

1. Proficiency in communication, reading and writing.

2. Ability to teach content area in Spanish.

3. Proficiency in and understanding of the student's vernacular.

4. A linguistic knowledge of both English and Spanish.

The scope of course offerings to develop language competence ranged from no courses, perhaps relying on courses offered in Modern Foreign Language Departments, to six courses (see Appendix C). Most of the courses were designed for students who already had oral communicative skills and thus emphasized vocabulary development for the teaching of subject content, composition, basic Spanish phonology and comparative English-Spanish linguistics.

The questionnaire circulated by the Institute for Cultural Pluralism to solicit specific competencies needed by teachers in bilingual-bicultural programs in general resulted in a reiteration of the competencies expressed by the conference participants. It was felt that in order to teach language arts in a language other than English, the teacher himself must have the skills he is to impart to the learner. He must possess:

1. Good oral-aural skills--i.e., be a native speaker or have near native proficiency.

2. A full command of the writing conventions of the language.

3. The ability to read the language with native comprehension of both direct meaning and inferred cultural meaning.

4. Proficiency and understanding of the student's vernacular.

5. A valuing of language differences and how language varies for different people as opposed to being deficient.

6. A sensitivity and understanding toward varieties of language dialects.

Many respondents felt that if the situation warrants, the student's vernacular should be used as the vehicle of instruction. It was also felt that bilingual teachers who teach content areas should know the terminology needed to teach concepts. The specialized vocabulary needed to teach the various content areas must be learned and internalized if the learner is to provide a good language model. In general, the most basic qualification for a Spanish medium teacher is the ability to speak, understand, read and write the language with a high level of expertise.

In the area of teaching English as a second language, it was felt that the teacher must be a good model of the English language and must have a knowledge of the

56

contrastive cultural and linguistic features of English and Spanish. It was the general consensus that a knowledge of the mother tongue would enhance the teacher's effectiveness but that complete fluency in the language other than English was not essential.

Culture

The current educational literature reviewed placed great value on the importance of the teacher's understanding of Mexican American culture. It was often stressed that teachers must be alert to the differences in languages, values, customs, and cultural heritage of the students. Teachers must understand their students feelings, attitudes, emotional responses and the fact that one way of life is not better or more deserving than another. Much of the literature attributed the failure of the school to reach the Mexican American student to the inadequate preparation of the teacher in the cultural characteristics, basic values and aspirations of the Mexican American culture.

Knowlton (1965) stated that because of the single culture orientation of most American schools, many Spanish-speaking students learn to regard their native language and culture as inferior to that of the Anglo-Americans. He suggested that a creative synthesis of southwestern cultures would produce classrooms in which the fullest potential of the Anglo-American, Mexican American and Native American cultures could be attained. The author viewed the monocultural school in a multicultural society as unrealistic and destined to continue to produce failures among culturally different students. A remedy in the form of multicultural, regionally relevant schools was advocated. Teachers must be responsive to the different cultural heritages, the different languages, and the cultural assets of the respective communities they serve.

Karr, Ken and McGuire (1970) were of the opinion that in order to advance the educational attainment of the Mexican American, higher education must prepare teachers who can deal with cultural, psychological and linguistic differences. They felt that, to be effective, a teacher needed training in understanding the dysfunctions between the values of the Mexican American culture and those of the Anglo culture and in counseling the particular difficulties of each group.

Ainsworth (1969) recognized that the teacher is the product of his own culture and his own professional and academic background, which have produced misconceptions that underlie many classroom practices and which have impaired teacher effectiveness when dealing with the culturally different student. He further stated:

Teachers preferably from Spanish speaking backgrounds should be trained in both Spanish and English. Historical origin and background, cultural characteristics and basic values and aspirations of the Mexican American culture as well as linguistics should be included in teacher education. School counselors should possess guidance skills to help solve Mexican American student's problems of role acceptance self-concept and social values.

In a report prepared for a conference in teacher education, Carter (1969) stated:

The so-called sociocultural content core is the most crucial for teachers of Mexican Americans and is also the area that is most slighted in regular teacher preparation sequence. Indeed it is appalling how few teachers are objective in their views of society and culture or have any real grasp of culture's influence on themselves or their students. This core must bear the burden of providing an objective understanding of:

1. The concept of culture and society.

2. Cultural evolution, social change, and the individual problem in coping with them.

3. The profound and perhaps all pervading influence of culture in determining human personality and behavior.

4. The concept of caste and subculture as they exist in the modern world, especially in the Southwest.

5. The nature and history of the diverse Mexican American groups and their cultures.

6. The role played by the school in transmitting the "general national culture."

7. The theoretical and practical aspects of problems related to cross-cultural schooling, especially vis a vis language differences and normative conflicts.

No teacher can succeed with the culturally different and/or poverty community unless some rather personal things occur. The student's basic assumptions about himself, the world he lives in, and his explanation of both must be subject to reappraisal. The "folk mystery" explanations of such items as race, achievement or poverty must be destroyed. Too often such unsound explanations deter an individual's ability to cope with the real problems associated with such ideas.

Angel (1968) viewed the present school policy as having had, and as continuing to have, damaging psychological consequences for the Mexican American student. He identified the area of teacher and administrative personnel preparation as one area where changes must be made. According to Angel:

Teachers of Mexican-American children must be especially prepared. The teacher who goes through the usual teacher preparation program is one who is presently in the schools and, in most cases, is quite unconsciously damaging the Mexican-American child psychologically; this includes the Mexican-American teacher as well as the Anglo.
The preparation programs for teachers of Mexican-Americans should include detailed knowledge of both Anglo and Mexican-American cultures, knowledge of the dynamics of transculturation, knowledge of how cultural processes operate in the cognitive and affective development of children, and "sensitivity-training" that will free the teacher from cultural ethocentrism on the one hand and allow acceptance of Mexican-American culture on the other. It is not enough to know about the culture; it must be felt.

Jaramillo (1972) reiterated and supported this belief by stating that programs dealing with bicultural education should offer more than the study of the culture (language, diet, costuming, socialization patterns, ethnics). She suggested going beyond this, basing her convictions on the fact that being bicultural implies knowing, feeling, and acting as a native of two given cultures. According to Jaramillo:

Biculturalism is a state that indicates knowing and being able to operate successfully in two cultures. Therefore a biculturate actually internalizes two modes of behavior in a given role which can be analyzed and utilized. He knows, is committed to, and has internalized the beliefs, values, customs, and mores of two different peoples. Bicultural education is the teaching of two ways of life.

Arvizu (1972) advised that we must learn from mistakes of others. Anthropologists and educators, he claimed, have historically been problem oriented and the possibility exists that perhaps anthropologists and teachers have contributed to the problems of ethnic minorities through their respective research designs and teaching strategies. He stated that contrary to the past patterns of negative approaches of anthropologists, resultant efforts need not adversely affect the group being given attention. The various branches of anthropology, encompassing physical anthropology, linguistics, archaeology, ethnology and applied anthropology can assist us in our task of looking at Mexican Americans in education. It can in Arvizu's words:

1. Outline and establish the Chicano way of life as valid and legitimate.

2. Add to the curriculum content and strategies which builds respect for differences.

3. Assist in training and retraining teachers more effectively.

Participants in the conferences related to bilingual-bicultural education reinforced the findings in current literature. The knowledge of the student's culture and the ability to internalize his culture here identified as essential. It was felt that only with these skills could a teacher present culture and cultural patterns without bias and interpret both cultures objectively. The cultural knowledge which a teacher should possess fell into three categories:

1. The artistic manifestation of the culture including art, music, dance, architecture, and crafts.

2. The socioanthropological facet of culture including history, geography, economics, philosophy, linguistics, religion, ethics and general socialization patterns.

3. The local cultural attributes the students bring to the classroom.

It was also suggested that the teacher should be cognizant of the contemporary life styles of the Mexican American and not be led astray by outdated life style comparisons made of the Mexican American in the past. Jaramillo (1972) reiterated this observation by stating that Mexican American culture is alive in the modern world and should be studied as such, instead of relying solely on its historical aspects.
The neglect of higher education in implementing programs of study which include courses that are culturally relevant to prepare teachers of Mexican American students was highly criticized. The recent report of the U.S. Commission on Civil Rights (1974) justifies this criticism. The Commission's review of college catalogues of 25 randomly selected southwestern institutions revealed that not one of the schools of education required trainees to take even one course in anthropology or sociology related to Mexican Americans, nor were the trainees required to take any courses in Mexican American history or culture.
The survey conducted by the National Bilingual Institute also measured the priority in teacher preparation for bilingual programs in terms of teacher's knowledge of children and appreciation of the cultural environment of their community. As Table 12 indicates, a high percentage (95 percent) of the respondents felt that a high priority should be given to the teacher's knowledge of children's cultural environment in the preparation for teaching in bilingual-bicultural programs.
The writer's survey of the existing university programs, shown in Appendix C, revealed the number of courses for cultural preparation ranged from one course to seven courses. Priorities in cultural training for bilingual-bicultural teachers were:

1. A knowledge of the historical, social, cultural and intellectual experience of the Spanish-speaking American in North America.

2. The ability to analyze the social forces which shape the behavior of the Spanish-speaking American.

3. A knowledge and understanding of intergroup ethnic relations in the economic, religious, familial, educational and political institutions of the United States.

4. A knowledge of pre-Columbian history.

5. A knowledge of the artistic contribution of the Spanish-speaking American to society.

The Institute for Cultural Pluralism's questionnaire on the specific competencies needed by teachers in bilingual schools in terms of culture identified the following competencies:

1. Knowledge of the contemporary life styles and culture of the Mexican American population.

2. Knowledge of the generic culture's historical and cultural development.

3. Sociocultural sensitivity-home and community based.

4. Knowledge of the cultural and historical development of the Mexican American.

5. Knowledge of the cultural and historical representation of the Mexican American.

6. An expanded awareness of self in relationship to culture--to one's own culture and other cultures.

7. A knowledge of how home and community environment affect learning behavior and styles.

8. A broad range of experience in the Mexican American population's community.

9. Exposure to psychological, sociological and anthropological theories.

10. A knowledge of assimilation process and its effect.

Professional Education

Current educational literature on the professional preparation of the teacher for bilingual-bicultural programs revealed that special competence is needed in the areas of:

1. Human development.

2. Learning theory.

3. Techniques of instruction.

4. Development of culturally relevant curriculum.

The area of human development involves giving children the opportunity to become constructively involved in developing their own personal effectiveness, self-confidence, and an understanding of the causes and effects in interpersonal realtions. A program based on human development principles capitalizes on the basic drives of children to achieve mastery and gain approval. In its broadest sense it is a strategy designed to improve communication between the teacher and the student and encourage a two-way flow of information between the students. In some ways this is the most important and perhaps the most ignored area in the education of the Mexican American. It is essential that attention be given in this area, especially at the secondary level, where the pressure on teachers to teach subject content tends to channel their attention to emotional development. Angel (1968) stated that it is at once a puzzle and a tragedy of democratic education, for such a central aspect of education to have been overlooked and little understood by educators even today. He further stated:

> One of the basic reasons why the affective development of Mexican Americans has been neglected lies in the lack of comprehension, by otherwise well meaning teachers, of what it means to be a member of a group whose way of life is different from the majority group. 'Children are children,' it is said. 'Treat each child as an individual.' 'I find that Mexican American students have the same needs as Anglo students.' 'Mexican American children are not different from Anglo children.' 'Don't emphasize differences, emphasize similarities.'
> Such comments, while praiseworthy from a democratic, ideological point of view, tend to pass over as relatively unimportant, differences in ways of life which sink down to the very root of behavior. This matter is not only misunderstood or misconceptualized by Anglo teacher and educator alone, but by many Mexican-Americans as well.
> It is of tremendous importance to understand the dynamics of acculturation, to begin to grasp what is involved. Being born into a cultural group that is different from the majority has consequences that are much deeper than discussions about democratic ideology or appreciation of another culture.
> Being born a Mexican American means that a child will learn about the world, that which the Mexican American culture teaches him. He will pay attention to things that his culture emphasizes. He will also learn to feel in certain ways about people, about events, about himself. He will learn certain food preferences, certain religious preferences, habits and ways of behaving in situations. He will develop certain attitudes about sex, about death, about the Anglo, in short, about all the important and unimportant aspects of living. He will become a Mexican-American, not an Anglo, not an Eskimo, not a German.

Ramírez (1970) expressed the need for teachers who can carryout strategies which can make the educational system more culturally democratic; that is, make the system more responsive to incentive-motivational, human relational and cognitive styles of Mexican-American students. He recommended the training of teachers who can implement the following classroom practices:

1. Usage of Spanish not only when curriculum is being presented but throughout the day and particularly when giving verbal reinforcement to the student so that both Anglo and Chicano students may associate positive feeling with the Spanish language.

2. A more personalized teaching style. Teacher interjects his personality (in terms of past experiences into his teaching strategy), and in addition, incorporates information he knows about the student's life style into the same strategy.

3. Achievement for the family. The teacher encourages the student to achieve so that his parents will be proud of him.

4. Cultural highlighting--the extent to which the teacher refers to Mexican-American culture throughout the school day, and even in aspects of the curriculum which might have no direct relevance to his heritage.

In his investigation Carter (1969) found that teachers lacked technical skills in the "science of teaching," that they were ill-prepared to use modern approaches to teaching English as a second language, that they rarely used technical equipment to its fullest potential, and that they did not have access to new and innovative materials in their teaching.

Angel (1968) has pointed out the lack of adequate teacher preparation for the teaching of Spanish in the classroom. Due to the large variance in language ability among Mexican Americans, the teacher must have a large reservoir of language teaching skills to adapt for each classroom situation and each individual student's needs.

In the area of preparing teachers and all educational personnel to develop relevant curriculum, Angel (1968) stated:

There is need for much curricular and instructional experimentation in educational programs for Mexican-American students. The special needs of Mexican American students call for more than "thinking" knowledge of curriculum and instructional development; they call for "feeling" knowledge as well. Elements of Mexican-American history and culture must be interwoven into curricular offerings for both Anglo and Mexican-American students. Whether curricular experimentation is to be in the hands of teachers or curriculum committees, both need to have training in curriculum development. A neglected aspect of curriculum development has been the lack of attention to the instructional activities that make content objectives realizable, especially in relation to the development of thinking objectives. Teachers, supervisors, administrators and central office personnel need training in these aspects of curriculum development.

In the area of reading and the selection of reading materials it is imperative that teachers be prepared to cope with the individual needs and interests of each student. Van Dongen (1972) stated that this emphasis on each student provided the opportunity to focus upon groups of children for whom reading instruction has not necessarily sparked interest, has not been meaningful, and has not provided opportunities for successful growth in skills, thinking and attitudes. Many Indian and Spanish-speaking students have experienced such frustration. Evaluation and selection of reading programs for these students must take into account the linguistic and cultural factors involved before, not after, the decision in selection is made.

The findings of such studies as those by Fisher (1968), Shirley (1969) and Williams and Edwards (1969) produced evidence that relevant materials can positively affect self-concept and have a positive effect on school achievement and school attendance.

An integral part of any teacher preparation program should be practice teaching. This component is particularly important for teacher trainees in bilingual-bicultural programs to enable them an opportunity to gain experience teaching Mexican American students. Jaramillo (1972) stated that field training should include the placement of teachers in schools where they could practice what they learned in their general studies and professional education. Teacher trainers must find ways to guarantee public school administrative support for implementation of innovative techniques and ways to place prospective teachers in schools with programs that they have been trained to implement. She stressed further that:

New teachers must become agents of change. A teacher possessing a thorough knowledge of the subject matter and all the techniques necessary for bilingual-bicultural education will surely fail unless he is well versed in the dynamics of social change. Any new curriculum or program that a teacher institutes will have repercussions at the administrative level and/or at the community level. The teacher must know the dynamics of social change if any of his ideas are to be implemented. He must be able, through his training, to establish the changes needed so that his new ideas can be put into practice. If the teacher is not trained to be a change agent, all of his other resources as a teacher are substantially weakened.

Participants in the conferences related to bilingual-bicultural education endorsed the professional competencies revealed in the literature. The professional competencies considered essential and fundamental covered a broad spectrum of skills including:

1. A knowledge of the rationale, the purposes or objectives and the content of the Spanish portion of the school's bilingual-bicultural education program.

2. Special methods and techniques useful in presenting content matter.

3. Language arts skills.

4. Ability to diagnose student needs and interests.

5. Planning of strategies in which the environment and the student interact for maximum linguistic and conceptual development.

6. Ability to select, modify, develop and use instructional materials.

7. The ability to present the values and ideals of the culture in a relevant, systematic, objective, and effective manner.

There is a dire need for colleges of education to provide teacher-training in the above areas. According to the latest report of the U.S. Commission on Civil Rights (1974) foundations and methods courses offered by teacher education institutions put little emphasis on specific information about the background and learning needs of the Mexican American student. For the 25 institutions whose catalogues were reviewed by the Commission fewer than one percent of the listed foundations and methods courses even mentioned the terms "Chicano," "Mexican American," "Spanish-Speaking," or "Bilingual," in their titles. None of the courses carrying these terms in the title or description were required courses.

The second survey conducted by the National Bilingual Institute measured the priority in teacher preparation for bilingual schools in terms of teacher's skills in the teaching process.

As Table 12 indicates a high percentage (85 percent) of the respondents felt the skills in the teaching process should be given a high priority in the preparation of teachers for bilingual programs.

The survey of existing university and college programs identifies the professional educational competencies as being:

1. An ability to rationalize and apply theory to practice in developing a bilingual curriculum (the designing, selecting, modifying, and utilization of materials in a bilingual setting.)

2. An ability to teach subject content in Spanish (science, math, social studies, language arts).

3. A knowledge of contrastive linguistics.

4. An ability to teach English and Spanish language arts.

5. Field experience in bilingual programs demonstrating teaching skills.

The Institute for Cultural Pluralism's questionnaire on the specific competencies needed by teachers in bilingual-bicultural programs in terms of professional education yielded the following competencies:

1. A comprehensive knowledge of recent research findings, available materials and curricula for bilingual teaching techniques and how to adapt and utilize these resources.

2. The ability to establish realistic criteria for performance in a bilingual classroom.

3. The ability to teach reading in Spanish.

4. The ability to devise strategies which are not culturally and linguistically biased which will lead to achievement of criteria specifically designed for culturally and linguistically different children.

5. Knowledge of a philosophy of education for the linguistically and culturally different.

6. The ability to utilize language assessment techniques as a training strategy and as a diagnostic tool.

7. An awareness of cultural pluralism as it relates to the schools, communities and the training of teachers and specialists.

8. A knowledge of skills in interpersonal effectiveness and personal development.

9. An awareness of how bilingual-bicultural influences affect and differentiate learning styles.

10. Familiarity with the strategies for educational reform.

School Community Relations

While community involvement was not an area of major concern some years ago, there is evidence of a growing dissatisfaction with the exclusion of the community from the educational process. Today's climate of awareness of social issues is generating activism on the part of a cross section of our communities which includes Mexican Americans, Native Americans, Blacks, Orientals and Middle-Class Whites who are demanding a voice and a legitimate role in the education of their children. Especially where a change or innovation such as bilingual education is being considered, the schools must now be prepared to deal with community feelings. Parents are no longer willing to accept major changes in educational activities without some interaction with the schools that satisfies their concern that the new way is the best possible one for educating their children.

Although emphasis on the need for community involvement is stressed in the current educational literature and supported by many bilingual-bicultural teachers, the tragic reality of the matter is that community involvement in bilingual-bicultural programs has not gone beyond the "biscochito" pusher (cookie pusher) syndrome. John and Horner (1967) stated that programs are often developed in isolation from the community and that parents' contributions are merely incidental.

Most writers on the subject advocate community involvement on the assumption that the schools have failed as a result of a lack of community participation. Community involvement is seen as a solution to many educational problems. Lopate (1968) stated that participation in decision making is widely accepted as inherently good. His hypothesis maintained that significant changes in human behavior can be brought about rapidly only if the persons who are expected to change participate in deciding what the change shall be and how it shall be done. Lopate also found the involvement of parents in school affairs to be positively related to their evaluation of the importance of education and their attitudes toward the school as an institution. Baca (1970) found that the use of adults or older youths in the classroom did much to enhance the continuity between the classroom and the community. Baca, former principal of Riverview Elementary School in Albuquerque, made good use of the school and community in this manner. Although this area is one of Albuquerque's most economically disadvantaged, Baca once had one of the largest and most active PTA's, Boy Scout troops, and community involved schools in the city.

This writer has concluded that an effective area which shows potential for enhancing the performance of low income and minority group children is the improved self-concept resulting from active parent participation in the schools. Thus, for the schools to be most effective, change is needed both in the schools and in the relationship between the school and the community. Education must become more relevant to the students and community and cultural integrity must be recognized.

Jaramillo (1972) felt that prospective teachers could learn much more in the community than they could in the classroom with professors who are not now "qualified" to teach. She advocated using community members from different walks of life (poets, artisans, community leaders, lawyers, etc.) who make more effective trainers for teachers than educators who have been involved solely in teacher training.

Ramirez (1970) recommended utilizing parents in the instructional phase of learning. He suggested asking parents to contribute resource materials for the heritage curriculum and enlisting their help in the actual teaching of other aspects of curriculum as well.

Participants in the conferences related to bilingual-bicultural education tended to identify competencies in community-school relations which fell within the realm of the cultural or sociocultural area. Although these competencies previously discussed are essential in creating an effective school-community relationship, this writer wished to isolate community school relations as a separate discipline which promulgates the direct participation of the community in the educational affairs of the schools. Having done this, the following competencies were identified:

1. The ability to provide opportunities for parents and other adults to engage in meaningful activities with the students.

2. The ability to provide children with opportunities to accept challenging responsibility in work and service in the schools.

65

3. The ability to create relevant curriculum through use of community ideas.

4. A knowledge and sensitivity to the community demands.

5. The ability to use community resource people in the diversification of classroom strategies.

6. The ability to identify community resources as possible entities for field trips.

7. A desire to become involved in the community.

8. A knowledge of group dynamics.

9. A willingness to carry out meaningful interaction with the community.

From the survey of the university programs it was quite apparent that institutions of higher learning have not yet taken a serious approach in the training of teachers to learning about the community and developing the skills needed to involve the community in the education of their children. The few universities that did offer courses concerning community based education emphasized the following teacher competencies:

1. Knowledge of communities where teachers will put into practice the skills they have acquired.

2. The skills needed to involve a community in the education of its children and in their own continuing education.

3. An ability to analyze the Spanish-speaking American experience in the United States, covering such topics as identity, housing, community organizations, employment, education and welfare.

The Institute for Cultural Pluralism's questionnaire on the specific competencies needed by teachers in bilingual-bicultural programs in terms of encouraging the direct participation of the community in the educational affairs of the school identified the following competencies:

1. The ability to plan and interact with the community.

2. Skills to develop roles that will form a bridge with the community.

3. A knowledge of techniques for establishing continuity between home and classroom and vice versa.

4. The ability to organize field trips to learn about generic culture.

5. A knowledge of local agencies that serve the Mexican American population.

6. A knowledge of the functions and relationships existing between the schools, other institutions and the community.

7. The ability to utilize paraprofessionals, community members, and community resources in classroom activities.

8. A knowledge of the techniques required to bring families of the economically deprived and culturally different into the school environment as active participants.

There are perhaps many other factors in the development of an effective community-school relationship. It appears safe to assume that the effective school of the future will be that which succeeds in creating an atmosphere that will provide for the educational, physical, social, cultural and emotional needs of children, youth and parents. It will receive strong support from the adults who are convinced that the objectives of the school are such that the total welfare of the community is served.

The survey of current educational literature, the consensus of conference participants, the survey of existing university bilingual-bicultural programs, and the Institute for Cultural Pluralism's questionnaire have revealed many of the competencies needed by a teacher in a bilingual program. The next chapter will present a program designed to develop those competencies considered fundamental for teachers who wish to work in bilingual-bicultural education programs on the secondary level.

CHAPTER VI

THE SECONDARY BILINGUAL-BICULTURAL TEACHER-TRAINING PROGRAM

Having identified the competencies considered essential for teachers in the bilingual school, this chapter presents a design for an undergraduate bilingual-bicultural secondary education program which will provide the prospective teacher with the necessary skills for working effectively in bilingual-bicultural programs in secondary schools. The program will be described in the following steps:

1. Rationale for the program.

2. General objectives of the program.

3. Specific objectives and minimum criteria of the program.

4. General description of the program.

5. Suggested courses for the program.

6. Suggested course descriptions.

Rationale

The proposed program provides for a subject matter specifically appropriate to secondary schools and bilingual-bicultural teaching situations. Its aim is to prepare teachers who will be sensitive to the linguistic and cultural needs of students enrolled in bilingual programs and who will be able to provide meaningful and satisfying learning experiences that will enable their students to develop to their highest potential in both languages and cultures.

In general the program will conform with the basic structure of undergraduate teacher education programs for secondary schools, including course work, field experience, practicum, hours of credit for graduation and certification, etc. Practicum will involve a partion of practice teaching conducted in schools with Mexican American students, under the supervision of teachers and professors who have demonstrated skill in teaching Mexican American as well as Anglo students.

Upon completion of the program, graduates will receive a B.A. Degree in Secondary Education with endorsement to teach in the bilingual-bicultural secondary school.

Prerequisites to bilingual eduation majors and minors are as follows:

1. Acceptance into a Teacher Education Program.

2. Students will be tested upon admission to determine their Spanish language competencies so that their program may be scheduled according to their linguistic skills.
    Transfer students will be placed according to the background which they bring to the program. The Spanish language courses offered in the program are language development courses and not Spanish foreign language instruction courses. Therefore, students who plan a major minor in Secondary Bilingual-Bicultural Education must have an oral-aural command of the Spanish spoken in New Mexico and the Southwestern United States.

The conclusion is that a teacher preparation program should be comprehensive enough to focus on all the recognized needs of bilingual students and should have continuity within this scope. Only when the prospective teacher has gone through the whole program can he be considered a finished product. Based on these assumptions and after careful analysis of bilingual educational needs, the following general objectives have evolved.

General Objectives of the Program

The general objectives of the program will focus on the four major areas identified earlier: language, culture, professional preparation and community-school relations. The major goal of the program is to produce competent teachers for English and Spanish-speaking students who are enrolled in bilingual secondary schools in the Southwest and, in particular, in New Mexico.

Language

Since the teacher will be working with English and Spanish-speaking students, he must have good communicative skills in the first and second language which will enable him to successfully teach language art skills to his students. The teacher must also have a knowledge of the functions and variations of regional and social dialects within language systems and be able to use the vernacular of the Mexican-American community in a manner which recognized its sociolinguistic requirements.

In addition, the teacher must know Spanish linguistic features and how they are contrasted with parallel features of English. He must have the ability to diagnose and evaluate individual language learning needs in a bilingual situation.

Culture

The emphasis in this area is to provide skills that will enable the teacher to communicate in a realistic manner with the Mexican American population. In order to accomplish this he must develop positive and comprehensive attitudes toward this ethnic group. To do so the teacher must have:

1. Knowledge of the current life styles and culture of the Mexican American population.

2. Knowledge of the Mexican American historical and cultural development.

3. Knowledge of the generic (Spanish and Indian) culture's historical and cultural development.

4. Knowledge of the historical and cultural contribution of the Mexican American people in the development of the United States.

Professional Preparation

This area builds upon the learning of the two previous areas and will aid the prospective teacher to develop:

1. The ability to view a culture from an anthropological perspective using a holistic, multi-disciplinary approach to the study of man.

2. The ability to view a culture from a psychological perspective.

3. A knowledge of skills in interpersonal effectiveness and personal development.

4. An awareness of how bilingual-bicultural influences affect and differentiate learning styles and how individualized instruction facilitates different learning styles.

5. A knowledge of how home and community environment affects learning behavior and studies.

6. The ability to establish realistic criteria for performance and/or behavior in a bilingual-bicultural classroom.

7. The ability to devise criterior-reference tests which approach a lack of cultural or linguistic bias to evaluate individual student's ability in terms of established criteria specifically designed for culturally and linguistically different students.

8. The ability to devise strategies which are not culturally and linguistically biased which will lead to the achievement of criteria specifically designed for culturally and linguistically different children.

9. A comprehensive knowledge of recent research findings, available materials and curricula for bilingual-bicultural teaching techniques and how to adapt and utilize these resources.

School-Community Relations

This area is developed concurrently and coordinated with the professional component. The course element is field centered and community based and will provide the prospective teacher with:

1. Field oriented experience of the functions and relationships among the schools, other institutions and the community.

2. The teacher must have the ability to utilize paraprofessionals, community members and community resources in the diversification of classroom strategy and facilitation of individualized instruction.

Specific Objectives and Minimum Criteria

The specific objectives of the program are related to the understandings, attitudes and professional skills that the prospective teacher should acquire during the educational process. The objectives for the four areas are expressed first as a general objective, followed by specific objectives and minimum criteria for achieving the objectives.

Language

A. The teacher must have effective communicative skills (comprehension, speaking, reading and writing) in his first and second language which will especially enable him to successfully teach the Spanish language art skills to his students.

Objectives	Minimum Criteria
1. Demonstrate ability to understand formal and informal Spanish	1. Listen to recordings (newscasts, narratives, etc.) of formal and informal Spanish and later paraphrase.
2. Demonstrate ar ability to understand directions in Spanish.	2. Carry out instructions in the use of audio-visual classroom instruction.
3. Demonstrate an ability to give classroom commands and directions.	3. Explain how to proceed from a certain position or place, to another place in the school, campus or neighborhood. Explain the reverse route.
4. Demonstrate an ability to communicate at the instructional level.	4. Verbalize the historical and cultural developments of the hispanic culture in the New World.
5. Maintain conversation in Spanish in informal conversational style.	5. Hold a conversation in an actual situation with a member of the Mexican American population.
6. Demonstrate the ability to communicate at a professional level.	6. Participate in a professional meeting of colleagues, give an address or announcement to a group of colleagues.
7. Demonstrate comprehension of material read independently in Spanish.	7. Answer questions about the content of a given passage.
8. Read material in Spanish and paraphrase.	8. Paraphrase a newspaper article covering at least 85 percent of the content.
9. Demonstrate an ability to present oral interpretations.	9. Present a five-minute reading of a prose selection, with proper use of (a) volume, (b) rate, (c) pitch, (d) gestures, (e) body movement and (f) mood changes.
10. Demonstrate clear, error free communication in the areas of spelling, punctuation, accentuation, sentence and paragraph construction.	10. Write from dictation, a simple paragraph. Write an original paragraph and progressively move to an original composition.
11. Demonstrate an ability to imitate in writing, models taken from literature.	11. Imitate the writing style of eminent Spanish, Latin American, or Mexican authors i.e. (Los de Abajo by Mariano Azuela).

B. The teacher must know the functions and variations of regional and social dialects within language systems and be able to use the vernacular of the Mexican American community in a manner which recognizes its sociolinguistic requirements.

Objectives	Minimum Criteria
1. Name characteristics of regional dialects in English.	1. Name at least 8.
2. Name characteristics of regional dialects in Spanish.	2. Name at least 4.
3. Name characteristics of social dialects in English.	3. Name at least 4.
4. Name characteristics of social dialects in Spanish.	4. Name at least 4.
5. Recognize dialect features in a given speech segment.	5. Given a recording, identify 8 different dialect features.
6. Identify sociolinguistic characteristics of language in the Mexican American culture.	6. Name at least 6 sociolinguistic features in Spanish and a means of using it. Include three examples from personal observations.
7. Demonstrate an understanding of language appropriateness criteria.	7. Discuss, describing at least 6 situations and giving examples for appropriate or inappropriate use of a particular dialect or style in speaking.

C. The teacher must know the linguistic features which comprise the Spanish language and how they are contrasted with parallel features of English.

Objectives	Minimum Criteria
1. Demonstrate understanding of the phonological system of English.	1. Match words from a list for which the vowel is the same; explain the principal difference in articulation of consonants between three pairs of similar words.
2. Discuss the phonological system of Spanish.	2. Explain the principal difference in articulation of consonants between 3 pairs of similar words.
3. Identify common instances of phonological interference between English and Spanish.	3. Name 6 examples, giving a reason for naming them; identify sources of difficulty in 10 given sentences.
4. Demonstrate understanding of the grammatical system of English.	4. Respond in writing to questions about the regularity of words and sentences of English.
5. Demonstrate understanding of the grammatical system of Spanish.	5. Respond in writing to questions about the regularity of words and sentences of Spanish.
6. Identify common instances of grammatical interference between English and Spanish.	6. Name 6 examples, giving a reason for naming them.

Objectives	Minimum Criteria
7. Demonstrate familiarity with current research and theory on Spanish language.	7. Discuss, summarizing at least 4 sources.

D. The teacher must have an ability to diagnose and evaluate individual language learning needs in a bilingual situation.

Objectives	Minimum Criteria
1. Diagnose the relative dominance of each of two languages for a given individual who is bilingual.	1. Given a recorded speech sample, name 8 examples which illustrate language dominance.
2. Distinguish between language problem areas which are related to development and those which are related to interference.	2. Given a recorded speech sample, name 4 examples.
3. Diagnose elements of bilingual interference in an individual's language performance.	3. Given a recorded speech sample prepare a language profile naming features of interference.
4. Identify language problem areas which are appropriate for instruction.	4. Given a language profile and recorded speech sample, name 3 appropriate language characteristics and give reasons for the choice.
5. Identify language problem areas which are not appropriate for instruction.	5. Given a language profile and recorded speech sample, name 3 inappropriate language characteristics and give reasons for the choice.

Culture

A. The teacher must have a knowledge of the current life styles and culture of the Mexican American population.

Objectives	Minimum Criteria
1. Identify and describe the values and attitudes of the Mexican American culture, and the degree of variation within the population.	1. Present through an appropriate medium 10 examples of the significant values and attitudes of the Mexican American population and the degree of variation among the population. (Significant values should be determined by class members.)
2. Identify and describe (a) the world view held by most members of the Mexican American culture, and (b) world views held by different members within the culture.	2. Present through an appropriate medium both (a) and (b), with 3 examples of how each is manifested in the culture.

Objectives	Minimum Criteria
3. Identify the principal features of the current Mexican American culture.	3. A final report on the principal features including commonly practiced holidays, customs, modes of dress, foods, folklore and other features deemed necessary by the instructor.
4. Demonstrate a knowledge of (a) the folklore of the Mexican American culture and (b) how they reflect the values and culture.	4. Present through appropriate media (a) and (b) to the satisfaction of the class members and the instructor.
5. Describe the function of the following relationships: parent-child, male-female, kinship, in the Mexican American culture, and name points of difference with their function in the dominant society.	5. Describe each to a degree of thoroughness to be defined by the instructor and name 3 differences across cultures for each.
6. Identify some current (a) artistic figures, (b) their works, and (c) how their works reflect the cultural experiences of the Mexican American culture.	6. Present through an appropriate medium (a), (b), (c) to the satisfaction of the class members and the instructor.
7. Identify (a) the current literary figures, (b) their works, and (c) how they reflect the cultural experiences of the Mexican American culture.	7. Present through appropriate media (a) (b), (c).
8. Identify the (a) current styles of music in the Mexican American population (b) significant musicians (c) how the music reflects the cultural experience of the Mexican American population.	8. Present through appropriate media (a), (b), (c) to the satisfaction of the class members and the instructor.
9. Identify the current mass media of the Mexican American culture, such as (a) magazines, (b) newspapers, (c) T.V. and radio programs.	9. Present through appropriate media at least 2 examples of each.
10. Identify (a) the current political figures and (b) the major social and political issues affecting the Mexican American culture.	10. Present through appropriate media (a) and (b) to the satisfaction of the class members and the instructor.
11. An awareness of personal reactions to the various cultural experiences.	11. Discuss personal reaction to the various cultural experiences including: (a) emotional experiences. (b) past experiences that have had an influence on present affective reactions. (c) possible influences on teaching effectiveness.

Objectives	Minimum Criteria
12. Describe sociocultural change in operation with a given community in the Mexican American culture.	12. Describe at least 2 examples, giving enough information for understanding by an individual who has never visited the community.

B.   The teacher must have a knowledge of the Mexican American population's historical and cultural development.

Objectives	Minimum Criteria
1. Identify the principal features of the Mexican American culture in the historic past.	1. Present through appropriate media the principal features of the Mexican American culture, including such elements as holidays, customs, modes of dress, foods, folklore, values, world view and any other element included by the instructor. Also present any changes that occurred in any of these elements over a period of time.
2. Identify major chronological events in the history of the Mexican American population.	2. Present through an appropriate medium the major historical events and the effects of these events on the Mexican American population and the Anglo American culture. Instructor evaluation.
3. Discuss the outstanding historical figures of the Mexican American population.	3. Present through an appropriate medium the outstanding historical figures and their contributions.
4. Discuss the prominent literary figures and their works.	4. Present through an appropriate medium a list of the prominent literary figures and discuss the significance of their works.
5. Identify and discuss the prominent aesthetic figures and their work.	5. Present through appropriate media a list of the prominent aesthetic figures and discuss the significance of their works or accomplishments.
6. Describe the past political and economic relationship between the Anglo American society and the Mexican American population.	6. Present through an appropriate medium the type of political and economic relationship that existed between the Anglo culture and the Mexican American culture and those events that influenced this relationship.
7. Describe the major cultural contributions to the development of the region.	7. Present through an appropriate medium 5 significant developments by the Mexican American population and the effects on the development of the region.

Objectives	Minimum Criteria
8. Describe the cultural influences of the Anglo American society on the Mexican American culture.	8. Present through an appropriate medium 5 significant cultural influences of the Anglo American culture on the culture of the Mexican American.

C. The teacher must have a knowledge of the generic (Spanish and Indian) culture's historical and cultural development.

Objectives	Minimum Criteria
1. Identify the principal features of historical generic (Spanish and Indian) culture.	1. Present through appropriate media the principal features of the generic (Spanish and Indian) culture, including such elements as holidays, customs, modes of dress, foods, folklore, values, world view and any other element included by the instructor. Present any changes that occurred in any of these elements over a period of time.
2. Identify major chronological events in the history of the generic (Spanish and Indian) culture.	2. Present through an appropriate medium the major historical events and the effects of these events on the generic (Spanish and Indian) culture, and the Anglo American culture. Instructor evaluation.
3. Identify (a) the current literary figures, (b) their works and (c) how they reflect cultural experiences of the generic (Spanish and Indian) culture.	3. Present through appropriate media (a), (b), (c).
4. Identify the (a) current styles of music in the generic population (b) significant musicians (c) how the music reflects the cultural experience of the generic (Spanish and Indian) population.	4. Present through appropriate media (a), (b), (c) to the satisfaction of the class members and the instructor.
5. Discuss (a) the folklore of the generic (Spanish and Indian) culture and (b) how they reflect the values and culture.	5. Present through appropriate media (a) and (b) to the satisfaction of the class members and the instructor.
6. Identify (a) the current political figures and (b) the major social and political issues affecting the generic (Spanish and Indian) culture.	6. Present through an appropriate media (a) and (b) to the satisfaction of the class members and the instructor.
7. Identify the principal features of the current generic (Spanish and Indian) culture.	7. A final report on the principal features, including commonly practiced holidays, customs, modes of dress, foods, folklore and other features deemed necessary by the instructor.

Objectives	Minimum Criteria
8. Identify some current (a) artistic figures, (b) their works, and (c) how their works reflect the cultural experience of the generic (Spanish and Indian) culture.	8. Present through an appropriate medium (a), (b), (c) to the satisfaction of the class members and the instructor.
9. Discuss the cultural influences of the generic (Spanish and Indian) culture on the English-speaking society.	9. Present through an appropriate medium 5 significant cultural influences of the generic (Spanish and Indian) culture on the Anglo American culture.
10. Describe the past political and economic relationship between the Anglo American culture and the generic (Spanish and Indian) culture.	10. Present through an appropriate medium the type of political and economic relationship that existed between the Anglo American culture and the generic (Spanish and Indian) culture and those events that influenced this relationship.
11. Identify and discuss the major cultural contributions of the generic (Spanish and Indian) culture to the development of civilization.	11. Present through an appropriate medium 5 significant developments by the generic (Spanish and Indian) population and the effects on the development of the region.
12. Identify and discuss the outstanding historical figures of the generic (Spanish and Indian) culture.	12. Present through an appropriate medium the outstanding historical figures and their contributions to the generic (Spanish and Indian) culture.
13. Identify and discuss the prominent aesthetic figures and their works.	13. Present through an appropriate medium a list of the prominent aesthetic figures and discuss the significance of their works or accomplishments.
14. Identify and discuss the values and attitudes of the generic (Spanish and Indian) culture, and the degree of variation within the population.	14. Present through an appropriate medium 10 examples of the significant values and attitudes of the generic (Spanish and Indian) culture and the degree of variation among the population. (Significant values should be determined by class members.)
15. Discuss (a) the world view held by most members of the generic (Spanish and Indian) culture, and (b) world views held by others in the generic (Spanish and Indian) culture.	15. Present through an appropriate medium both (a) and (b), with 3 examples of how each is manifested in the culture.

D. The teacher must have a knowledge of the misrepresentation concerning the historical and cultural contribution of the Mexican American population in the development of the United States.

Objectives	Minimum Criteria

1. Demonstrate a knowledge of the histori-cal representation of the Mexican American culture.

1. Identify in a standard text, news-papers, and/or other media, aspects of the Mexican American culture's history and culture which have been misrepresented.

2. Demonstrate an awareness of omissions of the Mexican American culture's his-torical and cultural contributions to the development of America.

2. Give examples of specific omissions of the Mexican American culture's contributions.

3. Demonstrate an awareness of current misrepresentation and omissions of the Mexican American culture's culture and history.

3. Give at least 5 examples of current misrepresentation of the Mexican American culture's culture and his-tory from at least 3 different sources such as textbooks, movies, T.V. etc.

4. Demonstrate an understanding of the effects of cultural and historical misrepresentation and omissions of members of the Mexican American popu-lation by members of the Anglo American culture.

4. Discuss the effects of cultural and historical misrepresentation on mem-bers of the Mexican American population and other ethnic popula-tions, including effects on self-concept, concept of other cultures, etc.

Professional Preparation

A. The teacher must have the ability to view a culture from an anthropological perspective using holisitc, multi-disciplinary approach to the study of man.

Objectives	Minimum Criteria

1. Describe man as a physical organism with human variations.

1. Include at least 12 physical charac-teristics and discuss how they vary among individuals, (a) interculturally and (b) cross-culturally, giving 4 examples each for (a) and (b). This information must be described in writing.

2. Describe culture as consisting of patterned ways of behavior which be-come unique to a particular society.

2. Use all of the following 6 factors: language, customs, beliefs, traditions, music and art. Give examples of all 6 for each of 3 cultures. Discuss 4 patterned ways of behavior: feeling, thinking, acting and talking as each one is unique to a particular society.

3. Describe ways in which culturally patterned behavior is learned from the group rather than being inherent.

3. Include 10 examples. List 3 differ-ent sources to support own. This may be oral or written.

Objectives	Minimum Criteria

4. Distinguish between biological and cultural adaptation to environment.

4. Give 6 examples of each. Examples must be specific to a given population. This may be done orally or in writing.

5. Describe the relationship between man's biological nature and man's preference for any one cultural trait over another. Determine whether the biological predispositions of man are imperative to culture.

5. Use 6 examples to illustrate own position. This must be described in writing.

6. Describe and critique current writings on variations in intelligence among individuals, as opposed to variations among races or cultures.

6. Give written descriptions of at least 4 articles published within the last 6 years on race and intelligence. The 4 sources must represent at least 2 different points of view.

7. Describe understanding of self as a member of a cultural group.

7. List and describe 6 factors which typify own culture. Discuss self in relationship to these. Oral or written description is acceptable.

8. Demonstrate an awareness of other cultures in relationship to one's own culture.

8. Discuss orally or in writing 6 factors of a culture other than one's own to which you have a favorable reaction, and 6 factors to which you have an unfavorable reaction. Give reasons for these reactions whenever possible.

9. Describe nonverbal responses toward members of another race which communicate positive or negative attitudes.

9. Give 10 examples. Include at least 5 examples from personal experience.

10. Discuss the nature of prejudice and its accompanying treatment, discrimination.

10. Include discussions of prejudice as prejudging behavior, and discrimination as related to fear of the consequences of reversal of the roles between the Anglo American and the oppressed culture. This may be oral or written.

11. Name customs (behaviors) that are common to every culture and show how they differ in 2 groups. For example: All people eat food. Anglos eat ham and eggs for breakfast, Mexican Americans eat huevos rancheros.

11. Include 5 examples which differ in 2 groups. These 2 groups may not be the same for all 5 examples.

12. Demonstrate an attitude of acceptance of other cultures as being different from one's own culture rather than as inferior to one's own.

12. Name two cultures other than one's own, and discuss 6 situations where one responds in the customary manner of that cultural group. Discuss each response in terms of the kind of response which could be typical of one's own culture in each situation described.

79

B. The teacher must have the ability to view a culture from a psychological perspective.

Objectives	Minimum Criteria
1. Discuss the commonly held stereotypes related to cultural groups.	1. Name 5 commonly held stereotypes related to culture groups.
2. Describe the stereotypes held by self.	2. Describe personal tendencies toward members of different cultures; include changes, if any, in personal feelings.
3. Identify current stereotypic statements occurring in a school.	3. Name statements heard in the school which were based on stereotypes.
4. Discuss the origin of specific cultural stereotypes.	4. Name and discuss the origin of 5 specific cultural stereotypes.
5. Discuss the manner in which cultural stereotypes are maintained.	5. Discuss the manner in which cultural stereotypes are maintained giving at least 3 examples of past occurrences and 3 examples of present occurrences.
6. Discuss the effects of stereotyping on teacher expectations of pupils.	6. List 5 effects of stereotyping on teacher expectations of pupils.
7. Discuss the effects of stereotyping on the self-concept of pupils.	7. Give at least 5 examples of the effects of stereotyping on pupils' self-concept.
8. Discuss the effects of stereotyping on pupils' learning.	8. Identify 5 effects of stereotyping on pupils' learning.

C. The teacher must have a knowledge of skills in interpersonal effectiveness and personal development.

Objectives	Minimum Criteria
1. Demonstrate a knowledge of self-awareness skills.	1. List and explain 8 of 11 ways to develop appropriate self-awareness skills.
2. Demonstrate an awareness of appropriate use of self-disclosure skills.	2. Show an acceptable rating level on a self-awareness inventory, after a series of group activities including: group, individual and instructor judgement. Give self-ratings from real-life situations.
3. Demonstrate a knowledge of the skills needed to develop and maintain trust.	3. Discuss the skills needed to develop and maintain trust, including at least 6 major points.
4. Demonstrate the skills used to develop and maintain trust.	4. Achieve an acceptable rating level on trust inventory, by group, self, and instructor after a series of group interaction activities, self-ratings in real-life situations.

Objectives	Minimum Criteria
5. Demonstrate an understanding of inter-personal communication.	5. Discuss, bringing out at least 5 of 7 basic elements of communication.
6. Demonstrate a knowledge of ways to improve the skills of sending messages effectively.	6. Discuss at least 3 ways a person can improve his communication. Discuss the concept of sender credibility, including at least 5 major elements.
7. Demonstrate knowledge of ways to improve listening and responding skills.	7. Discuss (a) 5 underlying intentions when responding, (b) the 4 dimensions of a message.
8. Discuss the characteristics of self-acceptance.	8. Bring out at least 7 of 11 characteristics.
9. Discuss methods to improve acceptance of self.	9. Name and describe 3 methods.
10. Demonstrate a knowledge of ways to communicate acceptance of others.	10. Discuss 2 major skills in communicating acceptance of others and 2 types of acceptance.
11. Demonstrate listening and responding skills.	11. Adequacy to be determined by ratings of instructor and the group after group interacting activity.
12. Demonstrate knowledge of constructive confrontation.	12. Discuss the following points concerning constructive confrontation: purpose, basic, rules, 5 types of confrontation. At least 6 of 8 skills must be involved.
13. Demonstrate constructive confrontation skills.	13. Rating by group and instructor after group interaction; self-rating after real-life situation.
14. Demonstrate knowledge of how to resolve interpersonal conflicts.	14. Discuss the following points: awareness of own conflict resolving style, 4 dimensions of conflict situation, 4 skills helpful in resolving conflict situations. Explain what constitutes conflict.

D. The teacher must have an awareness of how bilingual-bicultural influences affect and differentiate learning styles and how individualized instruction facilitates different learning styles.

Objectives	Minimum Criteria
1. Discuss how different cultural backgrounds present different learning patterns as a result of the following factors in a given culture: (a) values (b) traits related to success, (c) behaviors which are rewarded or punished, (d) handling of unacceptable behavior.	1. List 10 characteristic patterns of learning styles which distinguish children in the Mexican American population. Contrast these with learning styles in at least 4 other cultures.

Objectives	Minimum Criteria

2. Discuss how different linguistic backgrounds create different learning patterns and specific problems in language arts instruction.

2. Discuss the following: (a) language acquisition patterns of the Spanish language group, (b) contrastive linguistic patterns of Spanish and English language, (c) interference problems between the English and Spanish giving specific examples.

3. Describe the different linguistic abilities of bilingual children.

3. Describe at least five stages of bilingualism giving specific examples to illustrate description.

4. Discuss how cultural, regional, and social background affect the relevance of classroom materials and curriculum.

4. Utilizing a classroom text in area studies or reading, name: (a) specific incidences of vocabulary which culturally and linguistically different children will not understand, (b) professional and family roles described or pictured outside the experience of culturally and linguistically different children, (c) home and community activities outside the experience of culturally and linguistically different children.

5. Discuss how individualized instruction can deal with different learning styles and abilities.

5. Prepare a written rationale for individualized instruction which includes general strategies to deal with individual student's problems. Acceptability will be determined by instructor.

E. The teacher must have a knowledge of how home and community environment affect learning behavior and studies.

Objectives	Minimum Criteria

1. Discuss how family structure and roles affect attitudes toward learning and learning behavior.

1. Describe how each of the following affects learning attitudes and behavior: (a) attitudes toward elders, (b) number of siblings, (c) number and sex of parents, (d) older relatives in home, (e) patriarchal or matriarchal household, (f) family attitudes toward school and other community agencies, (g) economic conditions, (h) definition of kinship roles.

2. Discuss how community environment affects learning behavior and attitudes.

2. Discuss each of the following and how it affects children's learning patterns: (a) community attitudes toward public resources, (b) availability of community resources for children and parents, (c) contact with other children, (d) degree of familiarity of community members with one another (i.e. permanent population, or transitional). Acceptability determined by instructor.

Objectives	Minimum Criteria

3. Discuss how self-concept affects learning behavior and interpersonal
relations.

3. Discuss how positive and negative self-
concept affects learning attitudes
and behavior, giving specific examples.

4. Discuss how attitudes toward language
and culture are related to self-concept.

4. Discuss the following in terms of the
culturally and linguistically different child's self-concept: (a) attitude
at home toward the Mexican American
culture and language, (b) attitude in
the community toward Mexican American
culture and language, (c) proficiency
in Spanish and English. Acceptability
determined by instructor.

    F. The teacher must have the ability to establish realistic criteria for per-
formance and/or behavior in a bilingual-bicultural classroom.

Objectives	Minimum Criteria

1. Discuss the meaning of performance
criteria and the different kinds of
criteria.

1. Given a list of 10 items, specify which
ones represent statements of criteria
described in a list of 25 criteria
statements which contains all kinds of
criteria with 100 percent accuracy.

2. Differentiate between those skills
required for oral language performance and those skills required for
reading performance in the English
language and the Spanish language
(where applicable).

2. Discuss: (a) skills required for oral
language performance, (b) skills
required for reading performance, (c)
confusion over these two areas and
how it affects sequence of instruction.
Acceptability determined by instructor.

3. Demonstrate the ability to establish
criteria for oral language performance
in the English language for a bilingual child.

3. Given a hypothetical profile of the
language performance of a bilingual
student in a chosen grade, establish
criteria for oral language performance in the English language.
Acceptability determined by instructor.

4. Demonstrate the ability to establish
criteria for oral languages performance in the Spanish and English
languages for a bilingual student
(where applicable).

4. Given a hypothetical language profile
of a bilingual student in a chosen
grade, establish criteria for oral
language performance in the Spanish
and English languages. Acceptability
determined by instructor.

5. Demonstrate the ability to establish
criteria for reading performance or
reading readiness in the English and
Spanish languages for a bilingual
student.

5. Given a hypothetical language profile
of a bilingual student establish criteria for reading performance in the
English and Spanish languages.

6. Demonstrate the ability to establish
criteria for writing performance in
the English and Spanish languages for
a bilingual student.

6. Given a hypothetical language profile
of a bilingual student establish criteria for writing performance in the
English and Spanish languages.

Objectives	Minimum Criteria
7. Demonstrate the ability to establish criteria for attitudes of culturally and linguistically different students toward their own cultural heritage.	7. Identify what determines a positive attitude toward one's own culture; what determines identification with this heritage. Establish criteria for positive attitudes toward Mexican American culture. Acceptability determined by instructor.
8. Demonstrate the ability to establish criteria for skills in interpersonal relations among culturally and linguistically different students.	8. Establish criteria for skills in interpersonal relations among culturally different students. Acceptability determined by instructor.
9. Demonstrate the ability to establish criteria for positive self-concept of culturally and linguistically different students.	9. Identify what determines positive self-concept. Establish criteria for positive self-concept. Acceptability determined by instructor.
10. Demonstrate the ability to establish criteria for knowledge of Mexican American culture, history, customs, literature and art.	10. Establish criteria, giving reasons for each selection.
11. Demonstrate the ability to establish a series of intermediate criteria leading to an overall goal for a teaching unit in secondary area studies.	11. Develop and demonstrate teaching unit in secondary area studies. Establish an intermediate criteria giving a rationale for criteria established.

G. The teacher must have the ability to devise criterion-referenced tests which approach a lack of cultural or linguistic bias to evaluate individual student's ability in terms of established criteria specifically designed for culturally and linguistically different students.

Objectives	Minimum Criteria
1. Demonstrate a knowledge of criterior-referenced tests and how to construct them.	1. Discuss the advantages of criterion-referenced tests in a bilingual-bicultural classroom. Describe a criterior-referenced test. Construct a simple criterion-referenced test to measure specific hypothetical criteria.
2. Demonstrate a knowledge of what makes a test culturally or linguistically biased.	2. From an observation of at least 3 standardized achievement tests for elementary or secondary level, identify specific incidences of bias in the following areas: (a) vocabulary outside the experience of Mexican American culture, (b) family or professional roles outside the experience of Mexican American culture, (c) home and community activities outside the experience of Mexican American culture.

Objectives	Minimum Criteria
3. Demonstrate the ability to devise a criterion-referenced test to access students in area studies on the secondary level.	3. Given a hypothetical set of criteria for achievement in subject area studies, devise a test to measure achievement of criteria.
4. Demonstrate the ability to devise a criterion-referenced test to measure the level of performance in reading in the Spanish and English languages for bilingual students.	4. Given a set of hypothetical criteria devise a test to measure à bilingual students performance in relation to criteria.
5. Demonstrate the ability to devise a criterion-referenced test to assess skills in interpersonal relations.	5. Given a set of hypothetical criteria, devise a test to assess interpersonal relations of culturally and linguistically different students.
6. Demonstrate the ability to devise a criterion-referenced test to access level of oral language ability of a bilingual student in English and Spanish.	6. Given a set of hypothetical criteria for oral language performance in English and Spanish devise a test to measure performance.
7. Demonstrate the ability to devise a criterion-referenced test to access the level of reading ability of a bilingual student in English and Spanish.	7. Given a set of hypothetical criteria for reading performance in English and Spanish, devise a test to measure performance.
8. Demonstrate the ability to devise a criterion-referenced test to assess the level of writing ability of a bilingual student in English and Spanish.	8. Given a set of hypothetical criteria for writing performance in English and Spanish, devise a test to measure performance.

H. The teacher must have the ability to devise strategies which are not culturally and linguistically biased and which will lead to the achievement of criteria specifically designed for culturally and linguistically different children.

Objectives	Minimum Criteria
1. Demonstrate the ability to conduct a class in Spanish.	1. Conduct a half-hour class in subject area studies entirely in Spanish.
2. Contrast the techniques required for, (a) teaching English as a second language and (b) English as a first Language.	2. Identify 5 major differences in (a) and (b).
3. Contrast differences in teaching Spanish as a second language and as a first language.	3. Identify 5 specific differences.
4. Develop a series of instructional strategies which will enable a student to achieve established criteria in oral language performance in Spanish.	4. Establish hypothetical criteria. Construct activities for achieving the established criteria for a bilingual student whose first language is English; a bilingual student whose first language is Spanish.

85

Objectives	Minimum Criteria
5. Develop instructional strategies for teaching reading in English.	5. Establish criteria. Construct instructional activities for achieving criteria for a student whose first language is English; a student whose first language is Spanish.
6. Develop instructional strategies for teaching reading in Spanish.	6. Establish criteria. Construct instructional activities for achieving criteria for a student whose first language is English; a student whose first language is Spanish.
7. Develop instructional strategies for teaching writing in Spanish.	7. Establish criteria. Construct instructional activities for achieving the criteria for a student whose first language is English; a student whose first language is Spanish.
8. Develop instructional strategies for teaching writing in English.	8. Establish criteria. Construct instructional activities for achieving the criteria for a student whose first language is English; a student whose first language is Spanish.
9. Develop strategies to encourage students to verbalize in English and in Spanish.	9. Identify what skills students learn by talking, describing and recalling verbally.
10. Construct activities which will improve positive self-concept of linguistically and culturally different students.	10. Identify criteria for positive self-concept in group discussion and develop 3 activities.
11. Develop strategies for involving students in developing materials and planning instructional activities.	11. Discuss how students can contribute to their own learning; how they can express their own interests; how their interests can be used to develop curriculum and materials. Develop 5 strategies.
12. Establish criteria and develop strategies which are not culturally and linguistically biased, for a unit of work in subject area studies.	12. Justify one's own criteria in writing. Outline complete strategies for achievement of the criteria.

I. The teacher must have a comprehensive knowledge of recent research findings, available materials and curricula for bilingual-bicultural teaching techniques and know how to adapt and utilize these resources.

Objectives	Minimum Criteria
1. Demonstrate a knowledge of recent research in bilingual-bicultural teaching materials available and how to secure them.	1. Prepare a written report of current research and findings, including at least 4 sources, to be presented in class for other students.

Objectives	Minimum Criteria

2. Demonstrate a knowledge of existing bilingual-bicultural teaching materials available and how to secure them.

2. Describe at least 5 different materials and their sources.

3. Demonstrate the ability to utilize existing bilingual-bicultural teaching materials.

3. Perform a classroom demonstration of at least two different sets of materials.

4. Demonstrate the ability to determine the appropriateness of various materials for specific situations.

4. Given a hypothetical classroom situation, utilize information on students. Discuss advantages and appropriateness of one set of materials compared to others.

5. Demonstrate the ability to adapt existing materials to specific situations.

5. After examination of one particular set of bilingual teaching materials, revise the program to suit the individual needs of three students with different bilingual ability.

School Community Relations

A. The teacher must have field-oriented experience of the functions and relationships among the schools, other institutions and the community.

Objectives	Minimum Criteria

1. Discuss the structure of the school system in which he is involved.

1. Make a chart of the structural and actual status positions of the school personnel from the school board members to teacher aides.

2. Discuss the relationship between the school system and the achievement and academic performance of the students.

2. State the relationship between the school system and student performance and the several factors that may influence this relationship.

3. Identify the professional's general perception of the community.

3. Name the various views held by the professionals.

4. Identify the community's perception of the professionals.

4. Present the various community views of the professionals.

5. Identify the social service agencies which serve the school and/or the community.

5. Describe 5 social service agencies and how they serve the school/community.

6. Identify the social service agencies which could or should serve the the school and community, but don't.

6. Describe those social service agencies which do not serve the school/community but could or shouls, and the various reasons for this.

Objectives	Minimum Criteria

7. Discuss the community's viewpoint of the social service agencies and the services they perform.

7. Describe the various community viewpoints of the social service agencies and the services they perform.

8. Present the socioeconomic profile of the school community.

8. Include income levels, race, occupations, number of children and other features deemed important by the instructor or student.

9. Identify the major business establishments, the services they provide, and the cash flow which remains within the school community.

9. Present through an appropriate medium 10 major businesses and describe the services they provide and their cash flow.

10. Identify the key demographic features of the school community.

10. Describe the key demographic features of the community.

   B. The teacher must have the ability to utilize paraprofessionals, community members, and community resources in the diversification of classroom strategy and the facilitation of individualized instruction.

Objectives	Minimum Criteria

1. Discuss the training of paraprofessionals.

1. Describe preservice training of paraprofessionals; inservice training of paraprofessionals; and attitude of the school toward paraprofessionals.

2. Discuss the many roles which can be performed by the paraprofessional in a bilingual-bicultural classroom.

2. List ways in which a paraprofessional can expand the effectiveness of instructional strategies.

3. Demonstrate the ability to develop instructional activities to be used with a paraprofessional for effecting individualized instruction.

3. Devise at least 3 different approaches for team teaching with a paraprofessional to carry out individualized and group instruction in a bilingual-bicultural classroom.

4. Discuss the effect of parent participation in the classroom.

4. Discuss the relationship between parent interest and involvement and student achievement; how parent participation in classroom activities can expand cultural experience and the pride of students; and how parent involvement facilitates individualized and small group activities.

5. Identify community resources and agencies which can contribute to problem-solving within the school.

5. Discuss how agencies could be utilized effectively to aid individual students.

General Description of the Program

The intent of this program is not to determine the specific number of credit hours required in each specific component, but to prescribe a selection of courses in the different areas from which secondary education departments can draw after having administered a needs assessment of their prospective teachers. Through these courses and experiences the competencies of objectives and minimal criteria will be achieved.

As the program grows and develops changes may be necessary in the curricula and field-experience as indicated by appropriate, on-going evaluation. These changes should be instituted in an orderly manner as part of the ongoing teacher education program in the Department of Secondary Education and as part of the total structure of the College of Education. The program will consist of the following components:

1. General Education.

2. Subject Area Teaching Major or Minor.

3. Language.

4. History and Culture.

5. Professional Education.

6. School-Community Relations.

General Education: Courses which provide the prospective teacher with a rich background in liberal arts.

Bilingual Education Minor or Major Areas of Study: Courses in which prospective teachers propose to become competent in order to teach in the secondary school.

Language:

1. Spanish for Bilingual Teachers.

2. Spanish Composition.

3. Southwestern Spanish.

4. Comparative Linguistics for the Bilingual Teacher.

History and Culture:

1. The Mexican American.

2. Mexican American History.

3. Peoples and Cultures of Spain.

4. Artistic Development and Expression of the Mexican American.

5. Mexican American Literature for the Bilingual Teacher.

Professional Education:

1. Psychological Principles Applied to the Mexican American.

2. Methods and Materials of Bilingual Education.

3. Bilingual/Bicultural Curriculum Development.

4. Teaching Communicative Skills in English and Spanish.

5. Teaching Content Courses in the Bilingual School.

6. Oral Language Assessment.

School Community Relations:

1. Community Based Education.

2. The Mexican American Community.

3. Community Organization in the Mexican American Community.

Suggested Course Descriptions

Spanish for Bilingual Teachers.

A course designed to prepare the prospective bilingual teacher for oral expression, as well as developing reading skills and written exposition. Emphasis will be placed on building essential Spanish vocabulary and educational terminology used in the teaching of various subjects in a bilingual/bicultural secondary program.

Spanish Composition.

A course designed for students with a background in Spanish. It includes a thorough study of the sentence and its parts as a means of communication. Punctuation, accentuation, the mechanics of composition, the importance of dictation, variations in the Spanish language, and style in writing are developed through written exercises and class discussion. The course is aimed at encouraging the self-expression of the student.

Southwestern Spanish.

A course designed to sensitize the prospective teacher to the Southwestern Spanish dialect. A historical explanation of the archaisms, anglicisms, "pachuquismos," as well as a historical background for their uses. Clarification of the fact that Southwestern Spanish is a legitimate medium of communication and can be used as a means of instruction. Methods and techniques will be presented that capitalize on the regional dialect known by the students. This expands their knowledge of vocabulary so they can be functional in Standard Spanish as well as their own regional dialect.

Comparative Linguistics for the Bilingual Teacher.

A course designed to acquaint the teacher with the practical application as it pertains to the sound system, rhythm, juncture, pitch, stress, intonation, pronunciation and enunciation of the English and Spanish languages. Emphasis will be placed on the phonological, morphological and syntactic structure of English and Spanish along with an introduction of the language interference problem, dialectology and language acquisition.

The Mexican American.

A course designed to emphasize the culture, life styles, and social conditions of the present day Mexican-American. The impact of cultural and language differences and low economic status are treated at length. An analysis of the significant within group heterogeneity found in the Mexican American ethnic grouping will be conducted. Emphasis will be placed on within and intergroup ethnic relations in the economic, religious, familial, educational, and political institutions of the American society. Fieldwork in the Mexican-American community will be included so as to provide significant experiences for the students. Class materials will be related bilingually.

Mexican-American History.

A course designed to follow a historical approach to the social, cultural, and intellectual experience of the Mexican-American in North America. After a brief survey of the Spanish experience in Latin America, the course traces Mexican and Indian relationships between the Anglos and Mexican-Americans in the rural areas, small towns, and urban settings of the United States.

Peoples and Cultures of Spain.

A course designed to emphasize the cultural heritage of the Mexican-American from a historical and anthropological perspective. This course will be correlated with the course on the Mexican American.

Artistic Development and Expression of the Mexican-American.

A course designed to introduce the prospective teacher to Mexican-American drama, literature, poetry, art, music, dance, "fiestas patronales" and other arts. Guest lecturers will illustrate the artistic contributions of the Mexican-American people.

Mexican-American Literature for the Bilingual Teacher.

A course designed for acquainting the prospective teacher with material pertinent to the secondary level. Different facets, short stories, poetry, essays, novels, etc. will be presented stressing but not limiting the subject material to the Mexican-American area.

Psychological Principles Applied to the Mexican-American.

This course is designed to provide the prospective teacher with a systematic analysis of the forces which shape the behavior of the Mexican-American. The effects of prejudice and typical patterns of reaction to failure and lack of opportunity, the effect of poverty as related to life styles, compensation and over-compensation, and resulting value systems will represent the primary topics of concern.

Methods and Materials of Bilingual Education.

A course designed to provide fundamental training for prospective teachers intending to work in a bilingual secondary program which will provide comprehensive training in various facets of bilingual education. Topics include: a review of the structure of public education, definition and presentation of operational forms of bilingual education, bilingual curriculum materials, tests and measurements concerning bilingual students.

Teaching Content Courses in the Bilingual School.

A course designed to expose the prospective teacher to a variety of learning and teaching methods and techniques promoting an active learning process in teaching mathematics, science and social studies to the bilingual student. Competency will be established in understanding appropriate concepts and their relationships, conceptual schemes and processes and precise terminology in English and Spanish.

Teaching of Reading.

A course designed to focus on the development of a methodology for the teaching of reading to bilingual students, through the utilization of relevent Southwestern or Mexican American literature.

Oral Language Assessment.

A course designed to provide the prospective teacher with the skills necessary to conduct oral language assessment and determine dominance, comprehension, production, intonation and phonological and grammatical characteristics of students language. Emphasis will be placed on determining which student requires what kind of training and determining which pedagogical stretegies will best meet the individual linguistics needs of the student.

Bilingual/Bicultural Curriculum Development.

A course designed to aid prospective teachers to prepare their own curriculum responding to individual needs of Spanish-speaking students in bilingual-bicultural programs. Emphasis is given to the problems these students face in ordinary class-room situations so that they might be remedied by appropriate materials and activities.

Teaching Communicative Skills in English and Spanish.

A course designed to acquaint prospective teachers with different materials and methods for teaching the communicative skills to bilingual students. Emphasis will be placed on the aural-oral approach to language learning in both first and second language.

Community Based Education.

A course designed to provide the prospective teacher with skills needed to involve a community in the education of its children and in their own continuing education. Course work will consist of seminars, lectures, field trips to observe successful community projects and research into community dynamics. The course will be taught bilingually as many of the experiences will be at the grass root level in the bilingual-bicultural setting.

The Mexican American Community.

A course designed to study the migration of the Mexican American to urban settings, its sociological impact and problem of education, housing health services, family and community development. Practical experience and research will be a part of this course by placing students in agencies serving Mexican Americans.

Community Organization in the Mexican American Community.

A course designed to study basic community theory as applied to the Mexican American community using and analyzing case records. How are people motivated for self-help programs? Analysis of Mexican American organizations, their development, and the success of various techniques and approaches. Supervised fieldwork in organizations servicing a Mexican American clientele. Students will be assigned to a community organization.

CHAPTER VII

CONCLUSIONS AND RECOMMENDATIONS

A look at the educational profile of the Mexican American documented in this study illustrates the urgent need to re-align our educational system and focus more attention on meeting man's socio-educational needs. The place to bring about this change is in the teacher training institutions. Institutions of higher learning play a key role in instituting educational changes. It is these institutions that educate the people who will be entering the teaching profession and these are the persons to whom the education of the learner will be entrusted.

Only by bringing about a complete about-face in teacher training practices in our universities and colleges can we hope to realize an upward trend in the educational, social and economic profile of the Mexican American. For too long the educational attitude has been one that has produced ethnic isolation and linguistic rejection. The vicious circle of this persisting educational attitude has resulted in educational underachievement of thousands of Mexican Americans and other minority groups. It is this educational attitude that must change and replaced with a new philosophy--that of cultural democracy in education. The belief that the educational system be sensitive to the cultural unique personality of all Americans and respond by developing culturally democratic learning environments which are in harmony with those personal characteristics. This philosophy, then affirms the right of the culturally different individual to a bicultural identity. That is the right to maintain his identity with his ethnic group while he adopts values and lifestyles of the mainstream American-middle class. Given an enlightened educational environment the bilingual individual will find for himself the best of two worlds and will develop to his maximum potential in both.

With the continuance and proper articulation of bilingual-bicultural education in the secondary level with the now existing bilingual-bicultural programs in the elementary level we can rightly anticipate that we shall have in our secondary schools and colleges greatly increased number of students who have really mastered a second language. Mastery of a language way beyond the present stage of foreign language learning. By the time a full generation of bilingually-biculturally taught students has passed from the first to the twelfth grade; we shall have liberated second language learning from its foreign language syndrome and its present dependence solely on literary studies for advance work. We shall have given it full access to all other areas of the school and college curriculum. Finally, we can look forward eventually to a new kind of teacher in our ranks, a product of bilingual-bicultural schooling who has the competence that comes with familiarity from early childhood and through cultivation during his entire educational schooling.

Recently the Mexican Civil Rights movement has led social scientists and educators to question the validity of the educational attitude of our public schools and institutions of higher learning. It is indeed sad and tragic that in most cases they have merely been repeating arguments which George I. Sanchez had made more than a quarter of a century before. Nevertheless this new awareness is causing educators to seriously question some basic assumptions about themselves, school and American democracy. The movement for bilingual education, for example, is causing educators to examine their views of America as a monocultural-monolingual society. It is causing to question teachers' abilities in teaching linguistically and culturally different individuals, the validity of testing instruments used in the schools, the unrealistic portrayal of the Mexican American and Spanish involvement in past and present Southwest society and the cultural irrelevance in our present schools' curriculum.

Although the rectification of these points is not an answer in itself, it is however an important positive step in getting the schools geared into a new direction--schools that will serve students in much better ways, in much more humane and democratic ways.

The program designed to equip teachers with the skills necessary for the secondary bilingual-bicultural programs, hopefully will be useful to teacher training institutions in the Southwest. The specific regional differences and likeness as well as the needs of the specific population must be considered in determining priorities in different areas of the program. What has been designed is far from a perfect model for all geographical regions. The specific items must be determined on the spot. Regardless, it must be emphasized in conclusion that teachers must be prepared to cope with the responsibility of cross-cultural schooling. The school is charged with helping to solve grievious social problems. To do so requires a new breed of teachers, one equipped to make objective appraisals of problems, and to take rational and appropriate steps to encourage their elimination.

RECOMMENDATIONS

In view of the present status of bilingual education in the United States, the following would appear worthwhile.

1. Provide a systematic frame of objectives within which the effectiveness of this program can be assessed to determine how beneficial it is or can be. Even after the value of new techniques has been demonstrated and the techniques incorporated in their operating situation, their performance requires periodic monitoring.

2. A total commitment from the federal government for a stronger effort to assure equal educational opportunities in the Southwest.

3. Resolutions should be proposed and adopted in state legislatures in the Southwest urging colleges and universities to assume greater responsibility in training bilingual teachers.

4. State Departments of Education of the Southwest should modify teacher certification to require the type of teacher preparation specified in this study.

5. State Departments of Education should issue requirements that districts with students whose primary language is not English must provide teachers who speak the student's language and understand their cultural heritage.

6. Universities and colleges should implement teacher-training program for Mexican Americans and other minority groups as an integral part of their curriculum.

7. Increase Mexican American representation on staffs of institutions which control or influence teacher preparation programs.

8. An adoption of an affirmative recruitment program to increase the number of qualified bilingual teachers.

9. Encourage Spanish speakers to become teachers specialized in teaching in bilingual-bicultural programs. This would utilize a resource, bilingualism, already available to them.

10. Readapt teacher-training model presented in this study to use in inservice and retraining of teachers.

11. Investigation of materials presently being used in current secondary bilingual-bicultural programs before preparation of new ones is undertaken. Such investigation should be based on specific criteria.

12. Conduct a comparative study of students who have been exposed to bilingual-bicultural education from elementary to secondary and those who have been exposed to a monolingual-monocultural approach.

A DESCRIPTION OF SECONDARY BILINGUAL EDUCATION PROJECTS
FOR MEXICAN AMERICANS IN ARIZONA, CALIFORNIA,
NEW MEXICO, AND TEXAS

State, School, and District	Grade Level	Project Director	Project Characteristics
ARIZONA Phoenix Union High School, Phoenix School District	9-12	María Luisa Vega	Individualized classroom instruction, development of proficiency in subjects relevant to the student. Home visitations have proven helpful in creating a positive parent-community relationship.
CALIFORNIA De Anza Jr. High and Calexico High School, Calexico Unified School District	7-12	Harvey Miller	Bilingual Spanish and English education for students stressing teacher-oriented learning achievement packages. Program also includes a phase of test-development in an attempt to measure effectively language learning in English and Spanish. A high school organization, Estudiantina El Cid, gives students an opportunity to participate in a Spanish folk singing group.
CALIFORNIA Southwest Jr. High and Montgomery High, Sweetwater Union District	7-12	Paul H. Juárez	Major components are English and Spanish language development, self-concept development, and academic achievement. Program is geared to children of limited English-speaking ability who are new arrivals from Mexico or residents from low income families and English-speaking children who share the area's bilingaul-bicultural environment.
CALIFORNIA Coachella Valley High, Coachella Valley District	9-12	José P. Licano	Program gives students with limited English proficiency the opportunity for improved learning experiences, ESL, and normal progress at secondary level. English-speaking students may increase Spanish proficiency. Staff developed tests, workshops, innovative teaching systems and bilingual instruction are used.

A DESCRIPTION OF SECONDARY BILINGUAL EDUCATION PROJECTS (cont.)

State, School and District	Grade Level	Project Director	Project Characteristics
CALIFORNIA Gonzales Union High, Gonzales Union District	9-12	Eleanor J. Martin	Overall goal is an opportunity for students to improve acquisition of English and Spanish through special language classes and core curriculum courses taught bilingually. A supportive environment is provided for the non-English-speaker to prevent academic retardation. Self-concept development is vital. A Parent Advisory Council meets frequently to review progress, discuss policy and make recommendations.
CALIFORNIA King City High, King City District	9-12	Joaquín Chávez	Aim of program is the removal of the language barrier and the opportunity for students to function proficiently in two languages. Program also attempts to meet the educational, social and personal needs of the students, and thus provides knowledge that is relevant and immediately useful to each student.
CALIFORNIA McPherson and Portola Jr. High and Orange and El Modena High, Orange Unified District	7-10	Art Muñoz	Program's development is in the areas English, Spanish and Social Studies for non-Spanish-speaking Anglo students and non-English-speaking Mexican American students. Main efforts are to individualize instruction in the three academic areas in self-contained classrooms and to encourage parent and community involvement.
CALIFORNIA Oxnard and Channel Island High, Oxnard Union District	9	Madeline Miedema	Program stress proficiency in a second and understanding of Mexican and Southwest culture. Teachers are trained to teach bilingually in a modified flexible scheduling system with individualized instruction and team teaching. They are developing a bilingual, multicultural core curriculum for districtwide implementation.

A DESCRIPTION OF SECONDARY BILINGUAL EDUCATION PROJECTS (cont.)

State, School, and District	Grade Level	Project Director	Project Characteristics
CALIFORNIA Simons and Freemont Pomona Unified District	7-9	Ken Noonan	Program stresses a multicultural setting, speech, drama, parliamentary procedures, role playing language development, cultural heritage and involvement in social and political affairs. Student participation in school and community activities has increased, as has parent involvement.
NEW MEXICO Gadsden Jr. High, Gadsden District	7-8	Nonexistent	Program consists of courses in English as a second language.
NEW MEXICO Belen Sr. High Belen District	11-12	Joe García	Program includes courses in Hispanic culture taught bilingually and Spanish for the Spanish-speaker.
NEW MEXICO Zia and Alameda Jr. High, Las Cruces District	7	Elizabeth Horcacitas	Program includes courses in Social Studies and Science taught bilingually and Spanish Language Arts.
NEW MEXICO Robertson High, Las Vegas City District	9-12	Nonexistent	Program includes courses in Southwest Literature and Spanish American Culture taught bilingually and Spanish for the Spanish-speaker.
TEXAS Del Valle Jr. High, Del Valle Ind. District	8	George O. Head	Program is designed to meet the needs of children whose dominant language is Spanish, but it includes Spanish and English-speaking children.
TEXAS Alvarado Jr. High and Logan High, New Haven District	7-12	Clarence Wadleigh	Program goal is to create bilingual, bicultural citizens of the students. Development of each child's potential is stressed. Sensitive teaching, independent learning and diagnostic-prescriptive teaching are encouraged. Program hopes to create a model bilingual, bicultural community.

State, School, and District	Grade Level	Project Director	Project Characteristics
TEXAS Marshall Jr. High and Jeff Davis Sr. High, Houston Ind. District	9-12	Raúl Muñoz	Program develops and enhances student education through bilingual, bicultural experiences. In-service training programs and bilingual consultants are used to improve curriculum and teaching strategies. Parent involvement procedures are used. Domain observation checklists and cognitive rating scales enable teachers to identify attitudinal changes, achievement and problem areas needing special attention.
TEXAS Riverside, Corona-Norco and Alvord, Riverside District	7-9	David Bazán	Academic areas taught bilingually are Language Arts, Math, Science and Social Studies. Program is designed for children with limited English-speaking ability. Dominant English-speakers can learn a second language. Primary goals are to use dominant language to advance educational competence, improve self-concept and cultural pride; develop proficiency in English; preserve and extend use of Spanish; and produce greater community participation.
TEXAS St. Helena, St. Helena Unified District	9-12	Richard C. Roche	Program emphasized bilingual, bicultural experiences through curriculum of Spanish for the Spanish-speaker, ESL, Math in Spanish, Hispanic Heritage, and individualized tutorial and Folk Arts.
TEXAS Isabel Jr. High, Santa Paula District	9-12	Joe Bravo, Jr.	Program is a bicultural unit introducing historical, political and gastronomical factors

A DESCRIPTION OF SECONDARY BILINGUAL EDUCATION PROJECTS (cont.)

State, School, and District	Grade Level	Project Director	Project Characteristics
TEXAS L.J. Christen Jr. High, Laredo Ind. District	7	Evangeline Ornes	Consultants are utilized in staff development and as total project resources. Resource teachers use Piagetian-oriented intervention strategies. Acquisition of bilingual and other materials has been extensive. Project developed and adapted materials have been produced, some sommercially. Parent acceptance is high.
TEXAS Cooper, Rhodes, and St. Leo Jr. High and Lanier High, San Antonio Ind. District	10-12	Alberto Villarreal	Program has developed a multimedia learning system for Mexican American children.

Source: Guide to Title VII E.S.E.A. Bilingual Bicultural Projects in the United States, 1972-1973. (New Mexico projects identified by writer through visitations to projects or personal interviews with directors or principals.)

THE UNIVERSITY OF NEW MEXICO
COLLEGE OF EDUCATION
ALBUQUERQUE, NEW MEXICO 87206

Institute for Cultural Pluralism
Education Complex Rm. 117
Telephone: 505-277-3719   September 11, 1973

    I am in the process of researching the preparation of teachers for bilingual-bicultural education at the secondary level. The following information would be very helpful to me in initiating the preliminary phase of this study:

1. Name and mailing address of State Program
    Director for bilingual-bicultural education,
    if any.

2. Listing of state requirements for teacher
    certification in bilingual-bicultural education.

3. Names and addresses of colleges, universities
    and centers which have programs for the training
    of teachers for bilingual-bicultural schools.

    I would appreciate any consideration you may be able to give this request.

                  Sincerely,

                  Federico M. Carrillo
                  Director of Program Development

Survey of Bilingual-Bicultural Teacher Training Programs

State	Institution	Kind of Degree	Language Prerequisites	Instrument to Measure Prerequisite Skills	Lang.	Hist.	Cult.	Psy.	Socio-cult.	Phil.	Anthr.	Pol. Sci.	Fine Arts	Ling.	TESOL	Ed. Fdns.	Meth-ods	Prac-ticum	Com-munity
Colorado	Adam St. College	Undergrad., Specializing in Bilingual Education	Oral Language Mastery	Oral Exam	X	X	X	X	X	X			X	X	X	X	X		X
	Southern Col. St. College	Undergrad. Major in Bilingual Education	Knowledge and Understanding of Spanish Spoken in Mexico and the Southwest		X	X	X	X	X	X	X		X	X	X	X	X		
Connecticut	Univ. of Hartford	M.A., 6 Year Planned Program			X	X	X	X	X	X	X		X	X	X	X	X		X
	Univ. of Conn.	Courses in Bilingual Education				X	X	X	X		X		X	X	X	X		X	
Michigan *	Central Michigan Univ.	Major in Teaching Spanish-Speaking			X	X	X		X		X		X	X		X	X		
New York	St. Univ. of New York	M.A., Bilingual Education/TESOL	Competence in English and a foreign language		X	X	X	X	X	X				X	X	X	X	X	
	Hunter College	M.S., Education, Specializing in Bilingual Education	Proficiency in English and Spanish	Advisor Judgment	X		X	X	X	X				X	X	X	X	X	
	C.C.N.Y.	Bilingual Studies			X	X	X	X	X			X	X			X	X		
	Manhattan Comm. College	Bilingual Studies			X	X	X		X			X	X				X		
	Brooklyn College	Bilingual Studies			X	X	X		X			X	X			X			X
	Hostos Comm. College	Bilingual Studies				X	X					X	X						
New Mexico	New Mexico Highlands University	M.A., Bilingual Education			X	X	X		X					X			X		
	University of New Mexico	Composite Minor in Bilingual Education			X	X	X							X		X	X		
Rhode Island	Rhode Island College	M.A., Bilingual Education	Satisfactory Degree of Proficiency	Modern Foreign Language Department Judgment				X	X		X		X		X	X	X		X
Texas	Pan American Univ.	Undergrad Major	Proficiency in Spanish and English		X				X						X	X	X	X	
	Texas Womens Univ.	B.A. & Certification in Elementary Education	Proficiency in Spanish and English		X			X							X	X	X	X	
	St. Edward's Univ.	B.S. Elementary Education	Placement Test		X	X	X	X	X		X		X	X	X	X	X		
	Univ. of Texas at San Antonio	M.A., Bilingual Education	Proficiency in English and Spanish	Exam	X	X	X	X	X				X	X		X	X		
	Univ. of Texas at Austin	B.S., Concentration in Bilingual Education	Proficiency in Spanish		X			X	X					X	X	X	X	X	X

* Michigan: One semester of study in a Mexican University

APPENDIX D

CALIFORNIA STATE UNIVERSITY, SAN DIEGO
5402 College Avenue
San Diego, California 92115

Institute for Cultural Pluralism
17 November 1973

Dear colleagues:

The Institute for Cultural Pluralism at SDSU has been made responsibly by the School of Education for developing a proposal for the new California Bilingual/ Cross-Cultural Specialist Credential. We need a great deal of help, especially from educators like yourself who can provide a strong reality base and programatic suggestions.

Our immediate concern is to articulate competencies the BCC specialist should possess. Below are some examples from a District of Columbia program.

"Be able to communicate effectively in the languages and within the cultures of both the home and school."

"Understand the stages by which children acquire competence in their native language."

"Know and appreciate major dialectal differences in Spanish, and understand that there is no single variety which is 'better' or 'more correct' than another."

We solicit your competency suggestions on the accompanying questionnaire, as they relate especially your area of particular expertise--music, math, or whatever. Try to be more specific than the above examples, as we plan to use this information in making credential requirement decisions. Your insights will contribute in a very direct way to making the BCC credential an operational program by September, 1974. I thank you very much.

Yours sincerely,

Dr. M. Reyes Mazón, Assoc.Prof.
Director, Institute for
Cultural Pluralism

MRM/ep

104

NAME _____

SCHOOL AND DISTRICT _____

LEVEL _____

Suggested Competencies for
Bilingual Crosscultural Specialists

<u>Competency</u>   <u>Your Reason For Suggesting</u>

_____

_____

_____

_____

_____

_____

_____

_____

_____

_____

_____

_____

_____

_____

_____

_____

_____

_____

_____

_____

BIBLIOGRAPHY

Ainsworth, C.L. (ed.). <u>Teachers and Counselors for Mexican American Children</u>. Austin, Texas: Southwest Educational Development Laboratory, 1969.

Anderson, James G. and Dwight Safar. "The Influence of Different Community Perceptions on the Provision of Equal Educational Opportunities," <u>Chicanos: Social and Psychological Perspective</u>. Nathaniel N. Wegner and Marsha J. Hangs (eds.). St. Louis: The C.V. Mosby Company, 1971.

Andersson, Theodore. "From NDEA to EPDA: Can We Improve?" <u>Hispania</u>. 52, September, 1969.

Andersson, Theodore and Mildred Boyer. <u>Bilingual Schooling in the United States</u>. Vol. II. Austin, Texas: Southwest Educational Development Laboratory, 1970.

<u>An Evaluation of the National Bilingual-Bicultural Institute</u>. The National Task Force de la Raza, College of Education, The University of New Mexico, Albuquerque, New Mexico, 1973.

Angel, Frank. "Cognitive Development: A Neglected Aspect of Bilingual Education," From a book in preparation.

_____. "Program Content to Meet the Educational Needs of the Mexican American," Prepared for the National Conference on Educational Opportunities for Mexican Americans, April 25-26, 1968. Commodore Perry Hotel, Austin, Texas; Las Cruces, New Mexico: ERIC Clearinghouse on Rural Education and Small Schools, New Mexico State University, March, 1968.

Annual Reports Immigration and Naturalization Service, 1968-1972.

Aragón, Juan and Sabine Ulibarrí. "Learn Amigo Learn," <u>Personnel and Guidance Journal</u>. 50, October, 1971.

Arvizu, Steven F. "Anthropological Implication in the Education of the Mexican American," <u>An Emerging Design for Mexican American Education</u>. M. Reyes Mazón (ed.), Center for Communication Research, University of Texas at Austin, Austin, Texas, 1972.

Baca, Desi. "School and Community," <u>National Elementary School Principal</u>. Vol. L, No. 2, November, 1970.

Baratz, Joan C. "Teaching English in an Urban Negro School System," <u>Teaching English to Speakers of Other Languages</u>. Frederick Williams (ed.), Chicago: Markham Publishing Company, 1970.

Blair, Phillip M. <u>Job Discrimination and Education: An Investment Analysis, A Case Study of Mexican Americans in Santa Clara County</u>. New York: Praeger Publishers, 1972.

Burma, John H. <u>Spanish-Speaking Groups in the United States</u>. Durham, North Carolina: Duke University Press, 1955.

Carrillo, Federico M. <u>1972-1973 Follow-Up Report</u>. A Report prepared for New Mexico Highlands University on the Follow-up In-service Training of Bilingual-Bicultural EPDA Participants, May, 1973.

Carter, Thomas P. Mexican Americans in School: A History of Educational Neglect.
    New York: College Entrance Examination Board, 1970.

_____. "Preparing Teachers for Mexican American Children," A Report
    Prepared for the Conference on Teacher Education, New Mexico State University,
    Las Cruces, New Mexico, February 13-15, 1969. ERIC Clearinghouse on Rural
    Education and Small Schools, 1969.

Christian, Chester. "The Acculturation of the Bilingual Child," Modern Language
    Journal. 49, March, 1965.

Cooke, Henry W. "The Segregation of Mexican American School Children in Southern
    California," School and Society. Vol. 67, No. 1745, June 5, 1948.

Cordasco, Frank M. "Challenge of the Non-English Speaking Child in American
    Schools," School and Society. Vol. 96-5, No. 2306, March 30, 1968.

Demos, G.D. "Attitudes of Mexican Americans and Anglo American Groups Toward
    Education," Journal of Social Psychology. October, 1962.

Edmunson, Munro S. Los Manitos: A Study of Institutional Values. New Orleans:
    Middle American Research Institute, Tulane University, 1957.

Fernández, Pelayo. Teaching Spanish to the Spanish-Speaking Child, 1965-1968.
    Western Small School Projects for New Mexico, State Department of New
    Mexico, Santa Fe, New Mexico, 1968.

Fisher, Frank L. "Influence of Reading and Discussion on the Attitudes of Fifth
    Graders Toward American Indians," The Journal of Educational Research.
    November, 1968.

Fishman, Joshua and Erika Luders. "What Has the Sociology of Language to Say to the
    Teacher," The Functions of Language. New York: Teachers College Press,
    1973.

_____. "The Status and Prospects of Bilingualism in the United States,"
    Modern Language Journal. Vol. 44, March, 1965.

_____. "National Languages and Languages of Wider Communication in the
    Developing Nations," Prepared for Delivery as the Keynote Address at the
    Regional Conference on Language and Linguistics, Dar es Salaam, Tarzania,
    December, 1968.

Gaarder, Bruce A. "Challenge of Bilingualism," Published Under the Title of Foreign
    Language Teaching: Challenge to the Progession. A Report of the Working
    Committee II, Bishop G. Reginald (ed.), Northeast Conference on the Teaching
    of Foreign Language, 1965.

Gould, Betty. "Methods of Teaching Mexicans." Unpublished Master's Thesis,
    University of Southern California, 1932.

Guide to Title VII ESEA Bilingual-Bicultural Reports in the United States.
    Dissemination Center for Bilingual-Bicultural Education, Austin, Texas,
    1972-1973.

Heller, Cecilia S. Mexican-American Youth: Forgotten Youth at the Crossroads.
    (Studies in Sociology No. 20), New York: Random House, 1968.

_____. "Ambitions of Mexican-American Youth, Goals and Means of High School Seniors," _Dissertation Abstracts_, Vol. 25, No. 11, May, 1965.

Jaramillo, Mari-Luci. "Toward a Philosophy of Education for the Chicano: Bilingualism and Intellectual Development," _An Emerging Design for Mexican American Education_. M. Reyes Mazón (ed.), Center for Sommunication Research, University of Texas at Austin, Austin, Texas, 1972.

_____. "The Future of Bilingual Education," The University of New Mexico Albuquerque, New Mexico, 1970.

John, Vera P. and Vivian M. Horner. _Early Childhood Bilingual Education_. New York: Modern Language Association of America, 1967.

John, Vera P. "American Voices, Politics, Protest and Pedagogy," _The Center Forum_. 4-1-3, 1969.

Johnson, Kenneth R. _Teaching the Culturally Disadvantage: A Rationale Approach_. Palo Alto, California: Science and Research Associates, 1971.

Karr, Ken and Esther McGuire. "Mexican-American on the Move--Are Teacher Preparation Programs in Higher Education Ready," _A TESOL Bibliography. Abstracts of ERIC Publication and Research Report, 1969-1970_. Compiled by Anna Maria Malkoc, Washington, D.C.: TESOL Association, 1970.

Kayser, Jones Pauline. "The Role of Linguistics in a Bilingual Program for Teacher of Mexican-American and Migrant Children," _Teachers and Counselors for Mexican-American Children_. C.L. Ainsworth (ed.), Austin, Texas: Southwestern Educational Development Laboratory, 1969.

Knowlton, Clark S. "Bilingualism--A Problem or an Asset," _A TESOL Bibliography. Abstract of ERIC Publication and Research Report, 1969-1970_. Compiled by Anna Maria Malkoc, Washington, D.C.: TESOL Association, 1970.

Lambert, Wallace E. and Elizabeth Peal. "The Relations of Bilingualism to Intelligence." _Psychological Monographs: General and Applied_. Vol. 76, No. 27, Whole No. 546, 1962.

Lewis, Glyn E. Lecture on "Bilingualism and Bilingual Education in the Ancient World," Sponsored by the College of Education EPDA Programs for Training Pupil Personnel Specialist and National Task Force de la Raza, University of New Mexico, Albuquerque, New Mexico, 1973.

Lopate, Carol. "Decentralization and Community Participation in Public Education," _Review of Educational Research_. Vol. 40, No. 1, 1968.

Loretan, Joseph. "Evaluation of Science Instruction for Students of Spanish-Speaking Background," ERIC ED. 012-559, New York, 1967.

Mackey, William F. "A Typology of Bilingual Education," _Foreign Language Annuals_. III, No. 4, May, 1970.

Macnamara, John. _Bilingualism and Primary Education: A Study of Irish Experience_. Chicago, Illinois: Aldine Publishing Company, Edinburg, United Kingdom: Edinburg University Press, 1966.

Madsen, William. _The Mexican American of South Texas_. New York: Holt, Rinehart and Winston, 1964.

Malherbe, E.G. The Bilingual School: A Study of Bilingualism in South Africa. London and New York: Longmans, Green and Company, 1946.

Marland, Signey P. American Education. Health, Education and Welfare/Office of Education, Washington, D.C., Vol. 7, No. 1, January-February, 1970.

Manual for Project Applicants and Guarantees, Title VII. United States Office of Education, March 20, 1970.

Manuel, Herschel T. The Education of Mexican and Spanish-Speaking Children in Texas. Austin, Texas: The University of Texas Press, 1930.

_____. "Recruiting and Training Teachers of Spanish-Speaking Children in the Southwest," School and Society. Vol. 96, March 30, 1968.

Mayeske, George W. Educational Achievement Among Mexican Americans. A Special Report from the Educational Opportunities Summary Division of Operation Analysis, National Center for Educational Statistics, Washington, D.C.: Government Printing Office, 1967.

Meriam, Louis. The Problem of Indian Administration. Baltimore: John Hopkins Press, 1928.

Mittleback, Frank G. and Marshall Grace. The Burden of Poverty. Los Angeles: University of California, Mexican American Study Project, Advance Report 5, 1966.

Modiano, Nancy. "National or Mother Tongue in Beginning Reading: A Comparative Study," Research in Teaching of English, Vol. 5, No. 1, April, 1968.

Montiel, Miguel. "The Social Science Myth of the Mexican American Family," El Grito. 3, Summer, 1970.

McWilliams, Carey. North from Mexico. Greenwood Westport, Connecticut: Greenwood Press, 1948.

Nava, Julián. The Mexican Americans: An Anthology of Basic Readings (From the Beginning to the Present). New York: Vau Nostraud Reinhold Company, 1971.

New Mexico State Department of Education, Survey of Bilingual Education Programs, 1972-1973. Department of Communicative Arts, Santa Fe, New Mexico, 1973.

Obledo, Mario. Director, Mexican American Legal Defense Fund, "Hearings Before the Select Committee on Equal Education Opportunity of the United States Senate, Part 4: Mexican American. Washington, D.C., August, 1970.

Orata, P.T. "The Illoilo Experiment in Education Through the Vernacular," The Use of the Vernacular Languages in Education. Paris UNESCO, 1953.

Orstein, Jacob. "The Sociolinguistic Studies on Southwest Bilingualism--A Status Report," Southwest Areal Linguistics. Garland Bills (ed.), Institute for Cultural Pluralism, San Diego State University, San Diego, California, April, 1974.

Ortego, Phillip D. "Montezuma's Children," Center Magazine. November-December, 1970.

Parson, Theodore W. "Ethnic Cleavage in a California School." Unpublished Doctor of Philosophy Dissertation, Stanford University, 1965.

Pascual, Henry W. "Bilingual Education for New Mexico's Schools," New Mexico State Department of Education, Santa Fe, New Mexico, 1973.

_____. EPDA Proposal for Funding. New Mexico State Department of Education, Santa Fe, New Mexico, 1969.

Peña, Albar. "Teaching Content in Spanish in the Elementary School," Annual Conference, El Paso, Texas, November, 1970.

Ramírez, Manuel III. "Cultural Democracy: A New Philosophy for Educating the Mexican American Child," The Elementary School Principal. Vol. L, No. 2, 1970.

_____. "Identification with Mexican Family Values and Authoritarian in Mexican Americans," The Journal of Social Psychology. 73, First Half, October, 1967.

Rodríguez, Armando. Bilingual Education. Proceeding for the National Conference on Educational Opportunities for Mexican Americans, Held at Austin, Texas: Southwest Educational Development Laboratory, April 25-26, 1968.

Romano, Octavio C. "The Anthropology and Sociology of the Mexican Americans: The Distortion of Mexican Americans' History," El Grito, Fall, 1968.

_____. "Social Science, Objectivity and the Chicanos," El Grito. 4, Fall, 1970.

Romero, Fred. "A Study of Anglo Americans and Spanish American Culture Value Concepts and Their Significance in Education," Doctor of Education Dissertation, University of Denver, 1966.

Samora, Julián (ed.). La Raza: Forgotten Americans. South Bend: The University of Notre Dame, 1966.

Sánchez, George I. "An Interview with George I. Sánchez," The Elementary School Principal. Vol 1, No. 2, November, 1970.

_____. "History, Culture and Education," Chapter I in La Raza: Forgotten Americans. Julián Samora (ed.), South Bend: The University of Notre Dame, 1966.

Saunders, Lyle. Cultural Differences and Medical Care: The Case of the Spanish-Speaking People of the Southwest. New York: Russell Sage Foundation, 1954.

Shirley, Fehl L. "Influence of Reading on Concepts, Attitudes and Behavior," Journal of Reading. February, 1969.

Smith, Marguerite. English as a Second Language for Mexican Americans. A Report Prepared for the National Conference on Educational Opportunities for Mexican Americans, Held at Austin, Texas, April 25-26, 1960. New Mexico State University, Las Cruces, New Mexico: ERIC Clearinghouse on Rural Education and Small Schools, 1968.

Spolsky, Bernard (ed.), "The Language Education of Minority Children," The Language Education of Minority Children. Rowley, Massachusetts: Newbury House Publishers, Inc., 1972.

Steiner, Stan. La Raza: Mexican Americans. New York: Harper and Row, 1970.

Strom, Robert D. _Schools and Society_. Columbus, Ohio: Charles E. Merril Books, Inc., Columbus, Ohio, 1965.

Taylor, Paul S. _An American Frontier_. Chapel Hill: The University of North Carolina Press, 1934.

Tireman, L.S. "Bilingual Children," _Review of Educational Research_. Vol. II, June, 1941.

Ulibarrí, Horacio. "Cultural, Social and Socio-Psychological Variables in the Assessment of the Chicanito," The College of Education, University of New Mexico, Albuquerque, New Mexico, 1970.

_____. "Teacher Awareness of Socio-Cultural Differences in Multicultural Classrooms." Unpublished Doctor of Philosophy, Dissertation, University of New Mexico, Albuquerque, New Mexico, 1969.

_____. _The Spanish American: A Study of Acculturation_. College of Education, University of New Mexico, Albuquerque, New Mexico, 1969.

Ulibarrí, Horacio. _Educational Needs of the Mexican._ Unit of the Education Resources Information Center of the Bureau of Research, United States Office of Education, 1971.

Ulibarrí, Sabine. "Ulibarrí Habla," _El Hispano_. March, 1970.

United States Commission on Civil Rights, _Mexican American Education Study_. Report 1, Washington, D.C.: United States Government Printing Office, April, 1971.

United States Commission on Civil Rights, _The Unfinished Education_. Report 2, Washington, D.C.: United States Government Printing Office, October, 1971.

United States Commission on Civil Rights, _The Excluded Student: Education Practices Affecting Mexican Americans in the Southwest_. Report 3, Washington, D.C.: United States Government Printing Office, May, 1972.

United States Commission on Civil Rights, _Mexican American Education in Texas: A Function of Wealth_. Report 4, Washington, D.C.: United States Government Printing Office. August, 1972.

United States Commission on Civil Rights, _Teacher and Students: Mexican American Education Study: Differences in Teacher Interaction with Mexican American and Anglo Students_. Report 5, Washington, D.C.: United States Government Printing Office, March, 1973.

United States Commission on Civil Rights, _Toward Quality Education for Mexican Americans_. Report 6, Washington, D.C.: United States Government Printing Office, February, 1974.

Valencia, Atilano A. "Bilingual-Bicultural Education: A Prospective Model in Multicultural America," _TESOL Quarterly_. December, 1969.

_____. _Bilingual-Bicultural Education for the Spanish-English Bilingual_. Las Vegas, New Mexico: New Mexico Highlands University Press, October, 1972.

Van Dougen, Richard D. "Selecting Reading Materials--Student Concerns," Reading Strategies for New Mexico in the 70's. Resource Guide No. 2, Henry W. Pascual (ed.), Communicative Arts Unit, Division of Instructional Services. States Department of Education, Santa Fe, New Mexico, 1972.

Williams, Frederick D. (ed.). Language and Poverty: Perspective on a Theme. Chicago: Markham Publishing Company, 1970.

Williams, John E. and Edwards C. Drew. "An Exploratory Study of the Modification of Color and Racial Concepts Attitudes in Pre-school Children," Child Development. September, 1969.

Yarborough, Ralph M. "The Spanish-Speaking Child in the Schools of the Southwest," New Voices of the Southwest. Tucson, Arizona, October, 1966.

Yourman, Julius. "The Case Against Group I.Q. Testing," Phi Delta Kappan. 46-108-110, November, 1964.

Zintz, Miles U. Education Across Cultures. Dubuque, Iowa: William C. Brown Company, Inc., 1963.